Life Skills 101

Unchanged Life Principles

2nd Edition

By Kathi Boyle

ASA Publishing Corporation
1285 N. Telegraph Rd., PMB 351, Monroe, Michigan 48162
An Accredited Publishing House with the BBB
www.asapublishingcorporation.com

All Rights Reserved. No part of this publication may be reproduced, stored in a retrieval system or transmitted in any form or by any means electronic, mechanical, photocopying, recording or otherwise, without the prior written permission of the publisher. Author/writer rights to "Freedom of Speech" protected by and with the "1st Amendment" of the Constitution of the United States of America. This is a work of non-fiction Christian business education attributes. Any resemblance to actual events, locales, person living or deceased that is not related to the author's literacy is entirely coincidental.

With this title/copyrights page, the reader is notified that the publisher does not assume, and expressly disclaims any obligation to obtain and/or include any other information other than that provided by the author except with permission. Any belief system, promotional motivations, including but not limited to the use of non-fictional/fictional characters and/or characteristics of this book, are within the boundaries of the author's own creativity in order to reflect the nature and concept of the book. Unless otherwise indicated, most scripture quotations are taken from various biblical translations of the Holy Bible.

Any and all vending sales and distribution not permitted without full book cover and this copyrights page.

Copyrights©2024, Kathi Boyle, All Rights Reserved
Book Title: Life Skills 101 *Unchanged Life's Principles*
Date Published: 05.05.2024
Book ID: ASAPCID2380914
Edition: 1 *Trade Paperback*
ISBN: 978-1-960104-45-8
Library of Congress Cataloging-in-Publication Data

This book was published in the United States of America.

Table of Contents

Recommended 9-Week Teaching Schedule 1
Acknowledgments 5
Addiction: What is in control? 7
Adversity: Breeding ground for Miracles! 12
Anger Management: Take control 19
Attitude: How do you view the world? 25
Boundaries: Define your property 31
Budgeting: Manage what comes in and what goes out 40
Change: Changes that Heal 48
Choices: Decide what you want 54
Communication: Say what you mean and mean what you say! 60
Conflict Resolution: Conflicts happen when needs are not met. 68
Credit Repair: Keep your books in order. 74
Decision Making/Problem Solving: Know the next step 80
Emotional Intelligence: Use your feelings to your advantage 87
Forgiveness: Letting go of the baggage! 92
Goal Setting: Identifying what is important. 97
Job Readiness: How to interview 105
Love Barriers: Love as Jesus Loved 109
Organization: A place for everything 112
Personality Traits: Understanding yourself and others. 118
Relationships: Relationships determine your effectiveness 124
Risk Analysis: What is the cost? 130
Self-Discipline: Doing what you need to do when you need to do it! 135
Self-Perception: Seeing yourself as God sees you. 143
Self-Talk: Be nice to you 150
Success Principles: How to go to the next step 156
Time Management: Don't just spend it; invest it. 160
After Thoughts: 170

(Topics are listed in alphabetical order and are to be read in any order they may be needed.)

Life Skills 101

Unchanged Life Principles

2nd Edition

Recommended 9-Week Teaching Schedule
Class breakdown by week

Week 1:
1. **Addiction of WORRY!:** *What is in control?* Addiction holds you captive, keeps you awake at night, and blinds you to the possibility of the future. It does not mean you are a bad person; it means you have to work harder to be good, and the worst addiction of all is **WORRY!**
2. **Change:** *Changes that Heal.* People change when they hurt enough to have to; when they learn enough to want to when they know enough how to; and when they believe enough to be able to.
3. **Choices:** *Decide what you want.* We are right now exactly where we want to be in life. We are where we are because of the choices we have made; which means, we can be where we want to be by making different choices.

Week 2:
4. **Adversity:** *The breeding ground for Miracles!* Adversity grows character and increases faith. It takes you outside your comfort zone so you can grow.
5. **Attitude:** *The lens in which we view the world!* No matter how important your past was, it is not nearly as important as the way you see your future.
6. **Communication:** *Say what you mean and mean what you say!* Man is the only creature with the ability to think, plan, love, and speak. Communication occurs when the other person receives the message sent.

Week 3:
7. **Anger Management:** *Take control.* Anger is a natural, healthy reaction to emotions that tell us something in our lives has gone haywire. It is a defensive response to a perceived problem.

8. **Conflict Resolution**: *Conflicts happen when needs are not met.* Any time there is a choice to be made; there is an opportunity for conflict.
9. **Forgiveness**: *Letting go of the baggage!* Forgiveness means you will not allow the hurts of your past to damage your future. Because you forgive does not mean you forget, and because you remember does not mean you did not forgive.

Week 4:
10. **Goal Setting**: *Identifying what is important.* Goals are what wake us up in the morning and keep us moving through the day. Goals are the driving force to success.
11. **Decision Making**: *What is the best choice?* Decision making is limited by the information we have, the time we have to make it, and our mental ability to choose. Wise decisions are made by counseling with the wise.
12. **Problem Solving**: *Making the right decision.* Eliminate excess baggage; look to the past for lessons; and look to the future for opportunities.

Week 5:
13. **Personality Traits**: *Understanding yourself and others.* There is no such thing as a bad personality. There is good and bad in all of us. It is hurting people that hurt people.
14. **Relationships**: *Relationships determine your effectiveness.* "To get the full value of joy, you must have someone to share it with" (Mark Twain). Everyone you touch will pass along the results of being impacted by you.
15. **Thankfulness**: *Improve your happiness.* How one thinks about an event is more important than the event itself. The more thankful we are, the happier we are and the more energy we have.

Week 6:
16. **Self-Discipline**: *Doing what you need to do, when you need to do it, whether you want to do it or not!* The reason most of us fail to reach our full potential is because we fail to control our actions.
17. **Self-Perception**: *Seeing yourself as God sees you.* You can only give away what you have. If you don't love yourself, you cannot truly love another. Self-esteem begins at birth and grows or diminishes based on choices made.
18. **Emotional Intelligence**: *Use your feelings to your advantage.* What you feel is not as important as what you do with that feeling. Use what you feel to discern your situation and use those feelings to create opportunity.

Week 7:
19. **Job Readiness:** *How to interview*. Work is a large part of God's plan for our lives. Work is a form of love. The best moments in life will be when we know we have done a good job.
20. **Success Principles**: *How to go to the next step*. Success is the process of turning away from one thing to switch to something better. To get what you want from life, you must know what you want from life.
21. **Time Management:** *Time is not refundable*. You can spend it, waste it, or invest it, but you cannot return it.

Week 8:
22. **Risk Analysis:** *What is the cost?* The more you do, the more you fail; the more you fail, the more you learn; the more you learn, the better you get.
23. **Organization**: *A place for everything*. Organization is what you do before you do something so when you do it, it won't be all messed up. You can call it boring and difficult, but you cannot call it unrewarding or unimportant.
24. **Budgeting**: *Knowing where you stand.* Only when you measure what you have will you know what you need.
25. **Credit Repair**: Once the budget is set, getting the credit in line is critical to move forward.

Week 9:
26. **Boundaries**: *Define your property*. Your freedom ends where another's begins. Boundaries protect you from disrespecting others and them from disrespecting you. The goal of boundaries is to protect the one life God has given us stewardship over.
27. **Self-Talk:** We will believe what we tell ourselves before we will believe anyone else – including the professionals.
28. **Love Barriers:** So many things get in the way of relationships and "doing the right thing."

Acknowledgments

I would like to thank **Deborah Glass** for the years of motivation and encouragement she imparted into me. She is a true partner in every sense of the word. It has been a pleasure working with her.

To the hundreds of **students** over the years who have given me such great feedback and who have succeeded in their goals and dreams, thank you.

To my **children** (Kristopher Boyle, Jason Boyle, and Karen Smith) and to my surrogate son, Bob Kennedy, who have taught me most of the lessons I have learned and teach, thank you.

A special thank you goes to **Steven Hill of ASA Publishing Corporation** for his patients and kind leadership in getting this 2nd Edition published. I would highly recommend him for anyone interested in publishing a book.

But most of all, to my God. Without Him there would be no book. He continues to pick me up when I fall, hold on to me when I struggle, and work with me to complete each task He gives me. All the credit for all I do goes to HIM! My heart is HIS!

Kathi Boyle

Addiction *What is in control?*
Addiction is a physical and mental dependence on something, with an inability to stop using without a struggle.

What does Addiction do?

- It holds you captive.
- It causes you to lose control over your time.
- It keeps you awake at night.
- It prevents you from doing your best job.
- It causes physical and mental pain.
- It causes tension, fear, and dread.
- It distracts you from your responsibilities.
- It reduces your ability to focus.
- It blinds you to future possibilities.
- It forces you to focus on wrong things.
- It puts you under pressure.
- It prevents you from building relationships.
- It damages your body.
- It takes away your ability to laugh.
- It drains you of joy.
- It destroys your self-esteem.

When you look at the above symptoms you think of alcohol, drugs, and pills; but there is an addiction that is far more prevalent, more widespread, and equally or more harmful than any of those. As a matter of fact, more people are addicted to it than to all the other addictions combined **AND** it can keep you addicted to all other addictions.

What is this more potent and more prevalent addiction? **WORRY!** It causes every symptom listed above. In the Parable of the Sower, in the Bible, it is worry (birds, weeds, cares), that keep the good seeds from taking root. Worry can be a great reminder to practice letting go of the need to control outcomes. Statistics show us that 40% of all the things we worry about never happen; 30% of our worries are about things in the past that we cannot change; 12% of what we concern ourselves with is actually none of our business; 10% of worries are for imagined sickness; and 8% of our worries are for real problems that are outside of our control.

Some addictions happen because our bodies are allergic to the substance. Some happen because we feed them. But we always think we can control addictions. We never think it is as bad as it is portrayed to be. It deceives us. And we never, ever think it is going to happen to us. But it does. Amazingly enough, the most powerful addiction tool (*Alcoholics Anonymous*), against one of the most powerful addictions in the world, never asks people to decide to stop doing what is destroying their lives. Instead of mobilizing themselves, Alcoholics Anonymous followers are asked to **surrender** their wills. Try to overcome the problem by your will, and it will beat you. Surrender your will and sobriety becomes possible. Surrender, which we think means defeat, turns out to be the only way to victory. That is true of all addictions, including worry. Corrie Ten Boom, a survivor of the German Concentration Camps, said, *"Worry does not empty tomorrow of its sorrows, it empties today of its strength."* A day of worry is more exhausting than a week of work.

What is worry?

"Worry is wasting today's time cluttering up tomorrow's opportunities with yesterday's troubles" (Neil Clark Warren). Worry is an inordinate anxiety about something that may or may not happen. It is a joy-stealer. Worry is being concerned about things that are outside of our control - things we cannot change. It is being afraid before there is anything to fear. It is taking on responsibilities that do not belong to us. It is trusting in ourselves to be able to solve all our problems, when we know we are not in control in the first place.

When we stop worrying, we set the captive free. *"It is childish to play in the traffic of fear or let the hobgoblins of habit impede your progress"* (Charles Swindoll). Mark Twain said, *"I have had a lot of worries in my life, most of which never happened."* Worrying is like asking for what you don't want. *"Worry never robs tomorrow of its sorrow, it only saps today of its joy"* (Leo F. Buscaglia). Worry has a lot to do with how we view our Higher Power. Do we see Him as a Grandfather in the sky who allows us to get away with anything? As a Judge and Jury waiting for our mistakes? Or as a Guardian Protector who is training and guiding us through life's events? If we see Him as a Guardian Protector, we have no reason to worry. Our circumstances may be challenging, but God is not in Heaven wringing His hands trying to figure out how to protect us from them.

What is the cure for Worry?

The cure for worry is to free your mind to focus on positive thoughts (Philippians 4:8). Find a mentor to guide and direct you and accept that there can be peace in all circumstances, because all things have a seed of good in them, and that good usually comes from our response to bad circumstances. *"You cannot wring your hands and roll up your sleeves at the same time"* (Pat Schroeder).

When we focus on the wrong things (things we cannot control), we miss the main thing that life is all about – using our God-given talents. When we focus on the wrong things, we live our lives for the wrong reason. Be prepared to accept the worst that could happen, for when you prepare yourself mentally for the worst, it rarely happens; but, even if it does happen, it seems less challenging because you are better prepared for it. *"You will break the worry habit the day you decide you can meet and master the worse that can happen to you"* (Arnold Glasow).

The question is not, "Am I able to stop worrying?" The question is, "Am I willing?" Life will always be full of pressure. But Hudson Taylor gives us a wonderful way to look at pressure:

> *"It doesn't matter how great the pressure is. It matters where the pressure lies. See that it never comes **between** you and the Lord – then the greater the pressure the more it presses you to His Breast."*

One of the main worries many people have is that of getting old. *"How old would you be if you did not know how old you are?"* (Satchel Page). There is no choice as to growing older. The only alternative is the grave. The choice is not will we grow older; the choice is will we grow up? Maturity is a matter of choice.

What are the signs of Maturity?

If maturity is the goal, how can we tell when we have matured?

- Caring more for others than for ourselves.
- Sensing danger and evil before it happens.
- Having wisdom as well as knowledge.
- Controlling our emotions.
- Completing what we start.
- Changing, when we see a need to change.
- Doing what we need to do without supervision. Being self-disciplined.

- Bearing an injustice without looking for revenge.
- Smiling through adversity while looking for the miracles.
- Using the talents God gave us.
- Looking for talent in others.
- Being content with our circumstances as we work to improve them.
- Staying faithful through every challenge.
- Handling money with integrity and generosity.

The addiction of worry is a joy-stealer, and there are few joy-stealers more persistent than past memories that we refuse to release and fears that may never happen. God's specialty is bringing renewal to our strength, not reminders of our weaknesses. We are commanded not to worry. Therefore, if we do worry, we are breaking a commandment.

Create joy in your life. Laugh freely and laugh often, for laughter is the best medicine to cure any addiction. Read the book, <u>Laugh Again</u> by Charles Swindoll. Work is a cure for all worry.

Corrie Ten Boom, after losing all of her family in the German concentration camps, as well as much of her health, came out a free woman because of her faith and her attitude. Her philosophy was: *"Any concern that is too small to be turned into a prayer is too small to be made into a burden."* If you are going to pray, don't worry, and if you are going to worry, don't pray. Joy is a gift (John 15:11). Take it and smile.

Work is the cure for all worry.

God says, *"My Name is I AM."* Helen Millicoat wrote a poem, part of which I will quote:

> When you live in the past ...
> I am not there.
> My name is not I WAS.
> When you live in the future ...
> I am not there.
> My name is not I WILL BE.
> When you live in the moment,
> It is not hard.
> I am here.
> **My name is I AM!**

Addiction Questions

What is one thing in your life that you worry most about?

_____

_____

_____

_____

What is the probability that this incident will happen?

_____

_____

What is one thing you could do to prevent it from happening and to help relieve this fear?

_____

_____

Who do you know that you could discuss your concerns with that might have a solution?

_____

_____

_____

Work and exercise are two things that help to relieve stress and worry. What activity could you add to your life that might help you to stop worrying?

_____

_____

_____

_____

Adversity

Adversity is the breeding ground of miracles.
Without adversity no miracle is needed.

I have heard success in life comes not from holding a good hand, but playing a poor hand well. *"We can't change the cards we are dealt, only the way we play the hand"* (Randy Pausch, Professor Carnegie Mellon). Learning to deal with and conquer adversity is what makes us who we are. It draws out strengths and qualities that would not appear otherwise. L.L. Cool J says, *"When adversity strikes that is when you have to be the most calm. Take a step back, stay strong, stay grounded, and press on."* Adversity teaches us how to see, to change, and to grow. If we don't deal with adversity when it appears on our timetable, it will deal with us on its timetable.

Our bodies let us know when there is physical pain, and it expects us to eliminate it. Our brain, on the other hand, has a tendency to want to ignore mental pain and looks for defenses. When our heart gets involved, our head takes a vacation. Our nervous system craves predictability and stability from our environment. When we don't get it, we look for it elsewhere. One of the reasons we turn to substances or other addictions is to get relief from the stress of dealing with changes we need to make. When we feel a level of stress that appears to be unmanageable, we look for something that will help us to either slow down or speed up – and sometimes that something is a chemical.

It is easy to get caught up in self-pity, the "why me" syndrome, looking only at the unfairness of life; but when we do, we miss the lesson we are being taught. There are many causes for adversity, but the reason for adversity is not what is important. If we view adversity as punishment, we will fear it, resent it, and resist it. Adversity, regardless of the source, is God's most effective tool for growing character. Only the response to adversity is important. Our most common response is to ask the question, "Why?" When the question should be, "How should I respond?"

Adversity is inevitable in life. Misery is optional. Just as you prepare for war, prepare for problems. Have faith that everything will work out well, that there is light at the end of the tunnel, and that this, too, will pass. Adversity can create fear. Fear shows where your faith it. Is it in God or is it in us? Adversity is a teacher giving us an opportunity to see, to change, and to grow.

Let me give you a true story about how to handle adversity: A child was born three months prematurely. She was given a 1% chance of living and her parents were told, if she did live, she would never talk, walk, smile, or think on her own. Her parents said, "NO." They prayed for her, loved on her, and hovered over her.

Today, a few years later, she does walk, talk, smile (even teases), and thinks on her own. Her progress is slower than normal, and she may never be "normal," but her affect on this family is a greater blessing than if she were. I know. These are personal friends of mine. Prayer works.

For most people, this would be devastating. For this family, they still love each other, love life and their Higher Power. This is simply a challenge to prove the world wrong. They viewed their glass not as half-empty or half-full, but complete!

God used adversity to grow His people: Abraham was driven from home; Joseph was sold into slavery; Moses had to deal with stiff-necked people; Nebuchadnezzar was driven to the wilderness; and Paul was imprisoned.

If adversity is from God, the area where we are experiencing the most adversity is the area where we need the most work. For example: If greed or insecurity is a problem, financial stress may be the result. If pride is a problem, losing a position or family may be the result. Adversity, for God, is always aimed at growth. ***And those things that grow the strongest usually grow the slowest.*** People who look at adversity as a training ground are the wisest. They chose curiosity over self-pity or anger.

If we knew what to expect in the future, we would look at adversity differently. Some things are so important that they are worth God interrupting our happiness and health in order to accomplish them. If our response is right, our adversity will always benefit us and others; for nothing gets the attention of others like watching someone else suffer successfully. Sometimes our adversity is not for us; it is for the benefit of someone else.

When adversity is not for the other person and not a result of our own misbehavior, we have to assume it is an attack. Death, disease, famine, earthquake, war, addiction – these were not part of God's original plan. However, they are reality and we have to deal with them. We should not be surprised when we are treated unjustly. We should be surprised when we are not. We live in a fallen world. So, don't allow those who have hurt you in the past to continue to hurt you in the future. Let it go!

If we are not clear about the purpose of our adversity, we are subject to doubt. There is nothing more bewildering than doing what is right and watching things go wrong – DOUBT! Or experiencing adversity that is outside of our control – DOUBT! Or not being able to see the justice in the adversity – DOUBT! Satan's strongest tool is DOUBT! If he can make us doubt, he has our attention.

We cannot judge based on what we can see and hear. *"Every great man, every successful man, no matter what the field of endeavor, has known the magic that lies in these words: every adversity has the seed of an equivalent or greater benefit"* (W. Clement Stone). The circumstances and events that we see as setbacks are often the very things that launch us into intense periods of growth.

Adversity is a road to wisdom. **Wisdom is the ability to see things from God's perspective**. From His perspective, adversity is like surgery. When we submit to surgery, we are saying that our ultimate goal is health, even at the cost of pain. Adversity is a wonderful attention-getter. C. S. Lewis says, *"God whispers to us in our pleasure, speaks in our conscience, but shouts in our pain. It is His megaphone to rouse a deft world."* When nothing is wrong, we have the false assumption that everything is alright.

If you have adversity in your life that means something exciting is waiting for you. Often, as a parent, we struggle with discipline (adversity for our children) for fear that our child will not like us or we'll hurt their feelings. But the bigger fear should be: what will the child be like if he/she does not know there are consequences for misbehavior? All actions have consequences. God's concern is not that we like Him. His concern is that we BE like Him. Love necessitates the possibility and even probability of pain. **Adversity, no matter where it comes from, is what God simply allows to happen to us to prepare us for what He has for us.** When adversity is a result of our own behavior, there are several steps we need to take:

1. Assume responsibility
2. Ask forgiveness
3. Don't complain
4. Confront your weakness
5. Accept adversity as training
6. Thank God for the opportunity to grow

You can be sure, if the adversity comes from our Creator as discipline: 1) He wants us to know the "why"; 2) the discipline is connected to whatever it is He wants us to correct; and 3) God won't quit until He has made His point. His adversity is designed to take us to our roots, whether that root is pride, prejudice, selfishness, materialism, attitude, etc. If we allow adversity to work, we will make permanent changes. If adversity is taken from us, we will not grow. God's goal is for us to take on more than we can do by ourselves so He can get credit for the results.

Sometimes we have bad experiences just so we will be able to help someone else with the same challenge. It is only when we have been comforted that we learn how to comfort others, and the world is full of people who need comfort.

If something is hurting you, it's supposed to, and you need to do something about it! Discomfort that results in pain can be a key signal that we need to adjust how we think about and see things in our life - whom we should let or keep in our lives, and how we should make decisions about what to do next. As Benjamin Franklin said, *"Those things that hurt, instruct."* When Adversity hits, most people blame, deny, or have a pity-party. The proper response to adversity is faith, joy, and gratefulness for what it is accomplishing in our life. Adversity is a blessing in disguise (1 Thessalonians 5:16-18).

Life is like mountain climbing: fulfillment is achieved by relentless dedication to the ascent – sometimes slow and sometimes painful. There are three basic responses to adversity:

1. **Quitters**: Those who give up. They suffer far greater pain than they would by facing the issues. They are motivated by fear.
2. **Campers**: They only go so far. They are more comfortable with suffering than striving and are motivated by comfort.

3. **Climbers**: They understand setbacks are part of the ascent. They learn new skills to keep them moving forward. They are motivated by success.

Sometimes distance from a problem gives you room; the more space you have the more options you have; the more strategies you can employ. There is nothing cowardly about retreating; it is just choosing a better place to fight -- leave your ego at home. Bringing an ego to the fight is a bad idea. The way you deal with adversity will either allow you to be set free from headaches, confusion, guilt, and fear or allow you to be negatively affected in every aspect of your life.

Each time we respond to adversity, we learn something more about ourselves. We learn what works well for us, and what doesn't. This knowledge is incredibly valuable, both for handling the present crisis and for dealing with the next one that will inevitably come in the future.

"You have a choice of how to deal with adversity–how to respond to and deal with the challenges that you face each day. You either see them as obstacles or as opportunities. You either let them get you down or decide to overcome them" (Linda Adams, President of Gordon Training Int.).

When adversity comes, we can decide we are in the battle for our life, and it is not worth the fight. OR, we can decide we are in the battle for our life, and we are not going to lose. Is adversity a curse or a blessing for you? What we do with the events in our lives, determines the quality of our lives.

Benefits of Adversity

Adversity creates resistance. It makes you better if you don't allow it to make you bitter. We get very little wisdom from success. The problems we face and overcome prepare us for the difficulties in the future that we will face. When we eliminate our problems, we limit our potential. If you want to succeed, you have to learn to make adjustments to the way you do things and try again. In science, mistakes always precede the truth. If you can step back from the negative experiences you are facing, you will discover their positive benefits.

Trials improve our character. They provide growth opportunities on a faith adventure. Our human tendency is to avoid our responsibilities: to blame, complain, and justify. Handling trials requires that we accept our part of any problem. If our attitude is to look forward to what we will learn and what we will become because of them, then adversity is a blessing. We know from experience that testing improves patience and patience is a virtue.

"Our trials are a vehicle. We can lie down and let them roll over us and crush us, or we can climb in them and use them to take us where we should go. The trial becomes a chariot and we can have a translation from hell without to Heaven within. God's chariots (trials) are filled with love" (Anonymous). Satan uses adversity to harm us. We use adversity to excuse us. God uses adversity to grow our faith and character. The area where we are experiencing the greatest adversity is the area where God is working the hardest on us. If we knew the end from the beginning, we would look at our trials differently - and we would probably choose the path we are currently on.

"Though opposition and trials may come from without, it is a quality from within that determines the genuine response. . . It is an attitude of fortitude, forgiveness, rejoicing, peace and calm that relies on God despite the external circumstances." Bertram Melborne, PhD

You can either view adversity as a blessing or allow it to control your life!

Adversity of WORRY!

Looking back on your life, what is the biggest adversity you have faced?

_____

_____

_____

What aspect of your character improved the most from this event?

_____

_____

_____

How will you use this learning experience when you face your next adversity?

_____

_____

_____

Anger Management

If you are patient in one moment of anger,
you will escape a hundred days of sorrow.
Chinese Proverb

Anger is a **natural**, **healthy** emotion that tells us something in our lives has gone haywire. It has less to do with what happens to us than to what happens in us. It is neither good nor bad. It occurs as a defensive response to a perceived threat. **All** personalities get angry. The feeling is not the problem, but it becomes a problem when you allow it to hurt you or others.

Sometimes anger comes on quickly – before you have time to think. (Proverbs 14:17 *He that is soon angry dealeth foolishly...*) When this happens, your reaction will be whatever you have trained it to be; or, if not trained, you will react the way you have seen others close to you react. This is the reason it is so important to think about how you handle anger before it happens.

Some people express anger and some suppress it; neither works. If you express your anger inappropriately – either verbally or physically – someone gets hurt; and, in most cases, you later regret the lack of control. If you suppress anger, it does not go away; it builds. Depending on your personality - even if you never reach a point where you address the issue - it will take its toll on you physically and emotionally; sometimes in the form of depression, or headaches, or upset stomach, or even a heart attack. Unresolved anger does not fix anything.

Anger is expressed in many different ways. The way we most often associate with anger is harsh words or physical contact. Even though this reaction is painful and harmful, both emotionally and physically, it is not necessarily the worst reaction. There are many families that are estranged for years – and even sometimes for life – because the offended will no longer speak to each other. In many cases, anger shows up in passive-aggressive behavior – nice to your face but not nice behind your back - which includes backbiting and gossiping. Any form of uncontrolled anger is nasty. Sometimes aggressive anger will get what it wants; but no one respects a person who does not control their anger.

Strong-willed and powerful personalities (Choleric and Sanguine) are most likely to react with words or deeds. The withdrawn and laid-back personalities (Melancholy and Phlegmatic) are most likely to suppress their feelings and hold them inside. If you find anger building up, take a break. Go exercise – walk, run, hit a punching bag, do something physical. Physical activity stimulates brain chemicals and reduces stress.

Anger, **to be effective**, must be controlled. There are some basic principles to follow that help to control anger, and the first one is to never address an issue when the emotions are high. Take time to think things through. Count to ten (or 100 if necessary); but waiting overnight might even be better. Respond when you are calm and rested. Choose your words carefully. **The goal should not be to hurt, but to heal.** The main reason we often do not handle anger well is because we are looking at the person we are angry with as an object, rather than as an individual with feelings. When we recognize that the other person also has feelings, we will attempt to determine why they are hurt, scared, or embarrassed and, thus, deal with them differently.

Focus on solutions that work for both parties. Think before you speak and allow others to do the same. Stick with "I" statements – don't blame (even if there is reason to blame).   Stick with the subject – don't bring up past transgressions. If past transgressions keep coming up, postpone the discussion until all parties can agree to address one incident at a time. If any responsibility for the frustration rests with you, accept it and apologize – whether the other person does or not, and whether the other person accepts it or not. If you cannot come to an amicable solution, be willing to ask for help.

Things happen in life that should not happen. Hurting people hurt people – or even worse, people hurt people they care about. How you react will either perpetuate the pain or reduce it – not just for yourself, but also for those you care about. If an older brother violently responds to an injustice to his younger brother, he can leave the youngest brother (and parents and friends) without his presence when he has to pay for his reaction in prison. Then who takes care of younger brother?

One reason we react so strongly to injustice is because we fail to see that justice will be served, and we try to take on that responsibility for ourselves. If all we can see is human or earthly justice, we may be right. But all of us, at some point, will be judged based on our own behavior and that judgment will be fair.

Learn from every experience. At the end of each day, review the incidents of the day to determine how you handled them and how you could improve. What should you have done differently? What could you have done or not done, said or not said, that would have improved the outcome?

Hurting People Hurt People!

The problem is we cannot see the other person's hurt. We can only see their actions, and their actions are causing us or someone we care about to hurt. Anger is painful to the other person, but it is actually more harmful to the one who is angry. The stomach gets tight, the palms get sweaty, vision blurs, the heart pounds, the body tenses up, and adrenalin flows. This can lead to high blood pressure, digestive problems, sleep disorders, headaches, and even death. Is it worth it?

A study by the University of Michigan with Medunsa University in South Africa (2001-2002) – where most of the men have been subject to capture by one tribe or another in their lives – proved that forgiveness reduces the health effects of anger. How you react makes a difference in **your** life. Anger has less to do with what happens to you than it does with how you interpret and think about what happens to you. As you train yourself to think before you react, here are a few questions to ask yourself:

- Will my involvement change anything?
- Is this the best time or place to address the issue?
- Is the other party in a receptive mood?
- Can the other party hear what I have to say? Can they focus through their anger?
- How important is this issue to me?
- Am I the right person to be involved?

Start thinking about situations that always makes you angry. List the things you know trigger a reaction in you, and then put them in order of the most challenging to the least. What is your typical reaction to each issue? Make a list:

- Do you slam doors or throw things?

- Do you stomp your feet or hit things?
- Do you yell or say things you regret later?
- Do you get sarcastic?
- Do you back down or withdraw?
- Do you get depressed?
- Do you procrastinate?

Anger Symptoms to Watch for before the Anger:

- Tight Stomach
- Clenched hands or jaw
- Clammy or flushed hands/face
- Fast breathing
- Headache
- Unable to sit still
- "Seeing Red"
- Can't concentrate
- Pounding heart
- Tense shoulders

You cannot control another person's anger, but you can set your own boundaries as to what you will accept. Remove yourself from a person who is out of control (Proverbs 22:24). This is not cowardly. It protects you and it protects them. It is smart and logical; it is just plain common sense. Accept your responsibility, but don't take on the responsibility of others.

If the issue is worth addressing:

- Identify what you are really upset about.
- Pick a calm, quiet time to address the issue.
- Write out your thoughts before you go into the discussion.
- Know when to end the discussion.
- FORGIVE. FORGIVE. FORGIVE!

Aristotle said: *"Anyone can be angry – that's easy: but to be angry with the right person, and to the right degree, and at the right time, and for the right purpose, and in the right way – that is not within anybody's power and is not easy."*

So, when you enter conflict, do not assume you know what the other person is thinking or feeling. Don't use the words "always" or "never." Stay on topic; don't bring in past events. Keep your expectations reasonable. Be willing to apologize when necessary and to forgive when needed. Remember, our transgressions can cause others to fall (Deuteronomy 1:37), and other's transgressions can cause us to succeed (Genesis 45:5). Everything has its purpose. Other people are not the enemy. They may be the victims of their environment, but they are people who have been placed in your life for a reason. **There is no excuse for bad behavior!**

How do you retrain yourself?

Most conflicts come from a string of incidents that build on your emotions. When each incident occurs, if it is not managed as it comes up, the next opportunity to react will be stronger. So, how do you manage each incident? How do you train yourself to react properly (in an adult, caring manner) when your life goes haywire?

Think, in advance, of how you should react. What could you do in each situation to resolve the problem to your satisfaction without infringing on someone else's rights? Review in your mind incidents in the past where you have been angry. Relive them just as they happened. (This may make you angry again, but it is only temporary. So, stay focused.) Then re-visualize the incident the way you wish you had reacted. Think of the things you could have said to defuse the situation. Make this image real in your mind; then every time you think of this incident, think only of the new, revised scenario. This way, if this type of situation comes up in the future, you will find yourself reacting as you have trained yourself to react.

You cannot go backwards and change the past, but you can start now to train yourself to react differently in the future. Even though anger is a **natural, healthy** emotion, it is an emotional state that comes as a result of intense displeasure. Anger is a defense mechanism against fear, hurt or embarrassment. Even though you can't always control the situation you find yourself in, you can and should **ALWAYS** control your reaction to the situation.

"Be ye angry and sin not: let not the sun go down on your wrath." (Ephesians 4:26)

Anger Management

What is your typical response, or what physical symptoms does your body display to fear, hurt, or embarrassment?

_____

_____

_____

Think of one event in your life in which you reacted improperly and write down how you would act, if given a second chance. What would you change?

_____

_____

_____

All responses start in the mind. What thought process can you put in place now that will help you to have a more positive response to uncomfortable situations in the future?

_____

_____

_____

What is the most important lesson you have learned from your past responses to stress?

_____

_____

_____

Attitude
How You View the World?

Your attitude is how you look at life. Your view stems from your past, your present, and how you see your future. However, no matter how important your past may be, it is not nearly as important as the way you see your future. Your attitude determines your success in life. Whether we are depressed or joyful, at peace or in turmoil, it is not the goodness or badness of the world, but what is in our mind that affects the way we see life. The one thing that determines our potential, produces the intensity of our activity, and predicts the quality of the result we receive is our attitude.

Attitude is the lens through which you evaluate life. It consists of how we see ourselves, how we view others, and what we think of life in general. Ralph Waldo Emerson said, *"A man becomes what he thinks about all day long."* Do you expect things to go well or are you waiting for life to fall apart? It is a choice. There is a quote from Denis Kimbro's book, **Think and Grow Rich: The Black Choice**, that I think expresses attitude well:

"Our attitude determines whether we love or hate, advance or recede, succeed or fail. How incredibly unique it is that a God, who would create the complex and immense universe, would create the human race and give to those individuals the free choice that would permit them to select either their own achievement or their own destruction."

A negative attitude is like an infection, untreated it gets worse. Traits of a negative attitude include an inability to admit wrong, a failure to forgive, a critical spirit, a desire to hog credit, and a disease of ME (wrapped up in ourselves). Most bad attitudes are the result of selfishness – making no effort to help others feel good. The seven deadly sins are all attitude: pride, covetousness, lust, envy, anger, gluttony, and sloth.

What leads to a poor attitude? Attitude focuses on the emotional issues of our lives. It is not the experiences of today that drive people to distraction. It is the remorse or bitterness of something that happened yesterday and the dread of what tomorrow may bring. That is why we are to live one day at a time. Not doing what we know we should do causes us to feel guilty. Guilt leads to an erosion of self-confidence. As self-confidence diminishes, so does our activity. A lack of activity leads to a decline in results. As results suffer, our attitude weakens.

How we feel about things determines our attitude -- acting as if you feel a certain way can get the chemistry moving in that direction. "Fake it 'til you make it" is the right attitude to have. For whatever reason, it seems to be a human tendency to focus on obstacles and not on opportunity. When poor thoughts become chronic, they create hesitancy in trying new things, they diminish our self-esteem, they tarnish our self-image and they start a downward spiral toward a negative attitude. Control and be choosy about the thoughts you allow yourself to focus on. With the right attitude, we can move mountains. With the wrong attitude, we can be crushed by the smallest grain of sand. Your ability to reach your full potential will be determined by your attitude of "No, I can't" or "Yes, I can." For, in your mind, **what you believe to be true either is true or becomes true**. Weeds grow without any help. Flowers must be cultivated –nourished and protected.

Talent, experience, and willingness are not contagious - but attitude is. People have a tendency to adopt the attitude of the people they spend the most time with. Choose your associations carefully. Being around someone with a positive attitude is uplifting, motivational, exciting, encouraging, enjoyable, and contagious. To face trials in your life and win, you have to have a positive attitude. Your attitude will determine how far you go in life.

We are each born with unique talents, and those talents are only given to us so we can help others. What we are is our gift from God. What we become is our gift back to Him. Attitude is simply a decision we have made based on the life we have lived; and, since it is a decision, it can be adjusted through thought and action. The only way to become what you want to be is to think your way there. The only limitation placed on what you are able to achieve is your inability to recognize your potential and talent. Don't let your attitude be determined by your circumstances, but rather by how you view your circumstances. A grateful attitude does not develop by accident. It is a habit you create and work on.

Don't be held back by fear and caution. Memories affect our attitude. They either build up or tear down. When we think clearly, we are more likely to have a healthy attitude. Wrong thoughts may pass through our minds, but we don't have to give them room there. When going through hell, don't stop to take pictures. Keep moving. *"What lies behind us and what lies before us are tiny matters compared to what lies within us."* (Ralph Waldo Emerson). To drive fear away, help someone else. Encouraging others means helping them look for the best in themselves, and that process drives negative thoughts out of our minds. Hope is the only antidote for fear. Brian Tracy says, *"An attitude of gratitude is a step toward achieving something bigger and better than your current situation."*

Don't fail to venture out and try new things. Don't expect not to succeed. Remember to do all that you do with a **SMILE** (**S**how **M**ore **I**nterest and **L**ess **E**go). *"If you are not using your smile, you are like a man with a million dollars in the bank and no checkbook."* (Les Giblin). You are not going to become the light of the world by sitting back and glowing. You have to get out there and light someone else's candle.

Don't worry about criticism. Aristotle said, *"Criticism is something you can easily avoid by saying nothing, doing nothing, and being nothing."* You cannot avoid criticism if you want to be somebody. When you step out to embrace life, you find yourself coming alive. The secret to a positive attitude is happiness, and the secret to happiness is freedom, and the secret to freedom is courage – the courage to stand up for right and not fear the wrong in the world. You are a diamond in the rough that has been polished by the hard hits of courage you have faced. Life never grows great until it is tested, and happiness comes not from the outside but from the inside of you. No one else can make you happy or unhappy. That is your choice. No one can make you feel bad about yourself unless you let them.

Be grateful every morning that you have something to do – whether you want to do it or not. What you can do, you should do. Don't just sit there. Mark Twain said, *"Even if you are on the right track, you will get run over if you just sit there."* While you wait for luck to open the door, some determined soul with a "can-do" attitude will step ahead and open it himself.

We sometimes find ourselves stuck in the rut of mediocrity and stagnate; not because of our lack of potential, but because of our poor attitude toward our own success. Stay positive in adversity. *"It is not what you have lost, but what you have left, that counts."* (Chucky Mullins, Vanderbilt Quarterback). And Martin Luther King, Jr. said, *"Stand up. A man cannot ride your back unless it is bent over."* And Ephesians 6:13 says, *"Having done all . . . stand."*

Take a look in the mirror. There is no one in the world like you. You are unique –

therefore, how can you be inferior? Unique means you are not comparable. Attitude is how you think. Being optimistic means expecting the best and knowing you can handle the worst.

The right attitude keeps you going in the right direction. **There is no temptation to do wrong when you feel happy.** Get passionate. Be thankful. Thankfulness gives you peace and takes the sting out of adversity. It opens your heart and the hearts of others. It is not a magic formula. When you are thankful you cannot be worrying. Thankfulness and worry cannot fit in the same space.

You cannot fail with a good attitude, for the only failure is to not be the best YOU that you can be. Your attitude will determine how much you enjoy your success. There is no room in the present for the failures of your past. Even though others will use your past against you, God never consults your past to determine your future; so, don't poison your future with the pain of your past. The past is a school, not a weapon to be used against us. The past is given as a place to bury our mistakes. How efficiently we use the present is determined by our attitude about the past and our view of the future. The present gives us an opportunity to use the lessons of the past wisely. *"To endure what is, we must remember what was, and dream of things as they will be one day."* (W. A. Durant).

Vision is about being able to see what is in the future. Are you looking at the threats or at the possibilities? Are you able to see past the obvious and see the opportunity? That is a positive attitude. The courage to persist in times of adversity and disappointment is a key element in a positive attitude. Here are a few thoughts from some of histories greats:

"The only thing you have to give up to get what you want is your story about why you can't have it." (Tony Robbins).

"All that we are is a result of what we have thought. The mind is everything. What we think we become." (Buddha).

"It is never too late to become the person you could have been." (George Eliot).

"You will never reach the palace thinking like a peasant." (Denis Kimbro).

"Suffering is inevitable, but misery is an option." (Wayne Cordeiro)

*"Ability is what you are capable of doing and motivation is what you do. But, attitude

determines how well you do it." (Lou Holtz).

"We can complain because rose bushes have thorns, or rejoice because thorn bushes have roses." (Abraham Lincoln)

These are not the worst of times and they certainly are not the best of times. But, one thing is certain; it is the only time we have. (Paraphrase of a *Tale of Two Cities*)

"Watch your thoughts, they become words. Watch your words, they become actions. Watch your actions, they become habits. Watch your habits, they become character. Watch your character, for it becomes your destiny!" (Gandhi)

Your attitude influences what you think. What you think determines what you believe. What you believe influences the choices you make. What you choose defines what you are, and what you are attracts what you have. Therefore, your success or failure is dependent upon your attitude.

Each of us should be in a constant search for people we can admire and respect, books we can learn from, and seminars given by successful people; for in five years we will be exactly as we are today with the exception of the people we meet, the books we read, and the things we learn. Much of whom and what we are at this moment is a composite of the many people who have influenced us over the years.

Focusing on today and expecting a better tomorrow will lead you to a more positive attitude. You can let your setbacks be stumbling blocks or stepping-stones. Failure is not something that happens when you fall down. It is what happens when you refuse to get back up.

Attitude Questionnaire
How You view the World

What is the best thing about you?

_____

_____

_____

_____

What is one thing you could change that would make you think more positively about your abilities?

_____

_____

_____

Who in your life makes you feel good about yourself?

_____

_____

What is one goal you could set that would make you want to get up in the morning and, at the same time, lead you toward the future you desire?

_____

_____

_____

Boundaries
Identify the rules that apply within the framework of your life.

One of the best books I have ever read on Boundaries was by Dr. Henry Cloud and Dr. John Townsend, and the name of the book was **Boundaries**. In it they set forth the rules of engagement that protect us from disrespecting others and others from treading on us. Boundaries are not brick walls you cannot get over, but are rather fences or hedges that identify the property line. They have a gateway to let in the good and get rid of the bad. A boundary is a property line. It defines where you begin and where you end. You have an obligation to protect your property, but your rights only extend to your property line. Personal boundaries are the imaginary lines we draw around ourselves to maintain balance and protect our bodies, minds, emotions, and time from the behavior or demands of others.

The biggest challenge with boundaries is that most of them are set before we understand what they should be. They are set by those who raise us, by those who teach us, and by society itself. Then, as an adult, we are put in a position of having to re-evaluate and reset something we don't truly understand. We are, in effect, reaping what we have been sown. To say that one reaps what one sows is not a threat; it is a fact of life. However, reaping what we have been sown means we now have to weed and re-plant. Confronting irresponsible behavior in ourselves (or others) is not the painful part – consequences are; therefore, to stop the pain, we have to re-program. So where do we start?

Without healthy boundaries or with very weak boundaries, you simply **cannot have healthy relationships**. You give up a part of yourself to be available or accommodating; or you become so entangled with another person and their needs (co-dependent behavior) that you lose your own identity. This undermines your integrity and leads to a loss of self-respect — and the respect of those around you.

Emotions are a signal to us that something needs to be addressed.

- If we find ourselves controlling others or being controlled,
- if we find it difficult to have a good day,
- if loving or respecting others is a challenge,
- if our temper is out of hand or we give in too easily,
- if we find ourselves doing things because we feel we have to, rather than knowing it is the right thing to do,

These may be indicators that we have not set proper boundaries. This is an indication we need to re-evaluate and start over; for not setting boundaries will cause us to hurt ourselves and others. Boundaries are not only beneficial personally, but they are helpful for those we deal with. **If boundaries are not obvious, they are not fair.**

The main reasons most people do not set boundaries are simply because they have a fear of losing a relationship, a fear of not setting the boundaries correctly, and/or they do not recognize the benefit of setting boundaries or a combination of all of these. The ultimate goal is to free us to protect, nurture, and develop the one life God has given us stewardship over. Therefore, as we set boundaries, we need to look at our needs and analyze our talents to know how we can meet another's needs without hurting our own. Boundaries are a learned art. We have to make a few mistakes in order to learn how to set them properly. Trying and failing is not a problem. Failing to try is. Trying, failing, and trying again is called learning.

You, and only you, are responsible for your behavior. You have no control over another; however, you do have control over how you allow others to treat you. You have a responsibility not to support another's bad habits. You have a responsibility not to rescue someone from the consequences of their own behavior. When you rescue someone from their mistakes, you will just have to do it again (Proverbs 19:19). At the same time, you cannot use someone else's behavior as a justification for yours. You have a right to say NO and no obligation to say YES just because someone else demands it. To be passive is to support wrong. If you do not stand against, you automatically stand for.

To develop mature relationships with others, you have to set and know your own boundaries. We are responsible **TO** others but not **FOR** others. We are expected to protect ourselves from abuse, both intended and unintended. Boundaries help to do that. Let's use a well-known story of The Good Samaritan as an example of why boundaries are important. In the story, the Good Samaritan sees an injured victim and treats him, takes him to the nearest lodging, sets him up, and turns him over to the lodge-keeper. What if we change the story, and the Good Samaritan has no boundaries? He takes the injured man to the hotel and, the next morning, as he is ready to leave the man with the hotel management, the man says: "You can't leave me now. I still need you." So the Samaritan stays a few more days. Just as he is ready to go complete the work he had set out to do, he gets a message from the people he had planned to meet saying: "We could not wait any longer. We have sold our goods to someone else." Now the Samaritan has lost his potential income and his ability to pay for the man's needs – all because he did not set his boundaries to do what he could do and let someone else do their part.

So how do you know your boundaries are not properly set?

- Saying no when you mean yes or yes when you mean no.
- Feeling guilty when you do say no.
- Acting against your integrity or values in order to please.
- Not speaking up when you have something to say.
- Adopting another person's beliefs or ideas in order to be accepted.
- Not standing up to someone who mistreats you.
- Accepting physical touch or sex when you don't want it.
- Allowing yourself to be interrupted or distracted to accommodate another person's immediate wants or needs.
- Giving too much just to be perceived as useful.
- Becoming overly involved in someone's problems or difficulties.
- Allowing people to say things to you or around you that makes you uncomfortable.
- Not defining and communicating your emotional needs in your closest relationships.

When you have weak personal boundaries, every act of compliance, self-denial, or neediness chips away at your self-respect and the respect that others have for you. You are in a constant state of insecurity.

We have been so trained by society on what we "should do" that we feel unloving if we do not do what others are compelling us to do. We need to define our responsibilities and allow others to carry theirs. We need to take care of ourselves so we have the ability to care for others who are in need. Taking on someone else's responsibility is a form of controlling them and denying them the opportunity to grow. Behaviors have consequences. When we rescue someone from the consequences they should take on, we take away their opportunity to learn and grow. Don't pick up challenges God never intended you to carry.

So how do you set your own boundaries?

1. Mind Shift (change your mind). Begin with the mindset that having personal boundaries is OK. It doesn't mean you are selfish or unloving. It is both completely acceptable and absolutely necessary for healthy relationships. Understand that self-worth comes from defining your life as you want it to be, not from the acceptance or identity of others.

2. Define your values. Sit down and think about how you have been allowing others to take advantage of you and how you might be accepting situations that are really unacceptable to you. Make a list of things that you will no longer allow people to do to you, say to you, or do around you. Determine your need for physical and emotional space. Define your values, belief system, and outlook on life so you have a clear picture of who you are and how you want to live. Get very clear on that.

3. Communicate. Sit down with the people involved in crossing your personal boundaries and kindly communicate your mind shift. Let them know you have spent some time thinking about what is important and acceptable to you and what isn't. Let them know how they have crossed your boundaries in the past, and ask them to respect and support your new boundaries.

4. Expect resistance. Know that stating your boundaries will feel uncomfortable and difficult, especially if you are a pleaser. There may be some defensiveness and push-back from those involved. That's OK. They'll get used to your new boundaries over time. Be aware that some people in your life may fall away as a result of your outlook and demand for respect. But these may not be people you want in your life anyway. You will find you attract new, supportive, and healthy-minded people in your life. Whatever you do, don't compromise your values, integrity, and self-respect simply to keep someone in your life. Your soul can't sustain that.

5. Reinforce. It may take some time to train yourself and others around your new boundaries. Continue to reinforce them so that you are taken seriously and respected. Practice saying "no" when you are asked to do something you don't want to do. Create a plan for times when someone crosses your boundaries. Let them know what they are doing. Ask them to stop immediately. Walk away from any push-back or negative comments without acquiescing or getting angry. Over time, you and the other person will realize you are serious.

6. Reward with a thank you. Acknowledge and reward those who are supporting and respecting your personal boundaries. Thank them and let them know the positive impact it has had on your life. This will motivate them to continue their behavior.

7. Reciprocate. Understand that respecting boundaries goes two ways. Examine your own behavior and words to see where you might be crossing another person's boundaries. Work to change those behaviors so that you are reflecting the respect and support you want for yourself.

8. Stay Flexible. There's a difference between healthy boundaries and rigid boundaries. You don't want to be a controlling or dictatorial person. That's not the goal. The goal is a healthy relationship with those close to you, balanced by a sense of understanding, mutual support, and give-and-take. There may be occasions when you choose to bend your boundaries or allow someone to cross the line. When someone is hurt or sad, needs extra support, or asks for an exception with respect and kindness — these are times to show flexibility and love. As you gain confidence around your boundaries, you will know when and how to bend them.

9. Be Patient. If you have had weak personal boundaries for years, be aware that this change doesn't happen overnight. Disengaging from the emotions and beliefs that led you to weak boundaries requires practice, and sometimes it requires the support of a counselor or mentor. Begin to recognize and challenge the limiting beliefs that undermine your practice of setting boundaries. Try to require your boundaries be respected even when you feel unsure or uncomfortable.

10. Believe. Believe in yourself and your value as a unique individual who is worthy of love and respect. Trust your instincts and feelings about what you do and don't want in your life. No one knows better than you who you are and what you desire. Don't allow others to define that for you. Practice self-confidence and self-love until it feels natural. Setting and requiring boundaries is a great way to practice this.

You will find that fear diminishes significantly when you define and implement **personal boundaries** in your life. You will feel more empowered and self-confident because you are communicating your self-worth to those around you. The more you practice holding fast to your boundaries, the more love, respect, and support you will find in your life.

We are often better at setting boundaries that affect other people and disrespecting those we should set for ourselves. We regularly overstep our own boundaries in several areas: Eating, Money, Time, Work, Language, and many others.

EATING: From the beginning of time food has been used as a tempter. Food is not our comforter, nor is it our security, our gratification, or our pleasure; nor should it be a reward for good behavior or a punishment for bad. It is simply fuel for the body. We treat our pets and our cars better than we treat ourselves. We would not consider overfeeding or failing to feed our pet or operating our car without oil or gas. But we do it to ourselves all the time. Overeating makes us lethargic. Poor nutrition keeps our mind from performing at its peak. The biggest challenge with misusing food is that it is visible to the rest of the world. When we stop looking at our bodies and start looking at our souls and our hearts, our bodies will come in line. For over or under-eaters, food serves as a false boundary.

MONEY: Not controlling money puts us in a vulnerable position. Money problems result from several issues:

- Impulse buying
- Poor budgeting
- Living too high
- Credit card use
- Borrowing
- Poor savings
- Over- or under-work
- Enabling others

Often the problem with money is having no plan (no budget) and a need or desire for instant gratification. Patience really is a virtue where money is concerned. Think about a purchase overnight before spending. If we cannot say NO to spending, we can never reach a point of financial freedom. Money has become a status symbol (Idol) for many. Not having enough becomes a self-worth issue for men and a security problem for women. Borrowing, whether from credit card use or from friends, puts us in bondage. Decide how much you will give, how much you will save and live on the rest.

TIME: The most valuable gift you will ever be given is time. You are completely responsible for how you will spend it and how you will invest it. Managing time when you have more to do than you can do is critical. But, it is equally important not to waste your time when you have too much of it on your hands. Use your time to learn and grow and rest. The easiest way to learn is through others' experiences. Since many of those experiences are in biographies and autobiographies, read.

Set a specific time to get up and to go to bed so your body can learn to work on automatic and free your mind to relax when in bed and perform when awake. Create habits that save you time and allow you to be more productive.

LANGUAGE: This may be one of the most important boundaries you set. How we use language can seriously affect our relationships. The tongue is the source of both blessings and curses (Proverbs 18:21). It can be used to dominate a conversation, hide insecurity, gossip, threaten, or falsely flatter. Or it can be used to compliment, empathize, encourage, and motivate to make ourselves and others feel good.

Using inappropriate language reflects our character and diminishes our intelligence in the eyes of others. Allowing others to use poor language with us is an insult. Learn how to express yourself in such a way that respect is a natural result of your communication.

When boundaries are set incorrectly, how do we heal?

When we have poor boundaries, we cause someone else to suffer and pain becomes our teacher. Consequences are the only way to keep us from further damage. When dealing with someone who is hurting, boundaries are necessary for us and helpful to them. Be patient with yourself. We are often willing and quick to offer grace to another hurting person, but unwilling to accept our own limitations. Most boundary problems can only be cured with persistence, determination, and prayer. Trying to solve our problems by only dealing with the symptoms, usually leads to more symptoms. We have to get to the core. Where did the incorrect boundary come from? What steps do we need to take to correct it? Will correcting it cause hurt or harm?

There is a big difference between hurt and harm. If you have a toothache and go to a dentist, the cure will hurt but it will not harm. When you correct a bad boundary, sometimes someone will get hurt; but, in the long run, they are not harmed and neither are you. We have to learn to say NO: NO to poor relationships, NO to laziness, NO to poor self-talk, NO to over or under eating, NO to overspending, and NO to giving up. NO is not a bad word.

Don't be afraid to fail. You are only a failure if you fail to learn from the event. To solve any problem, you must be willing to fail. To learn you must continue to practice, complete what you start, not get distracted, and let go of excuses. You are a far greater example by falling and getting back up than if you never fell at all.

WE ALL HAVE CHOICS:

You do not choose for others, only for yourself. If your boundaries cause another to leave, it is very likely that that relationship was not the best for you to begin with. Forced affection is not affection at all. God says we are to give. He does not say we are to give whatever someone else demands of us!

If there are no consequences when boundaries are violated, no lesson is learned and poor behavior is reinforced. Establishing and maintaining boundaries is a very difficult job. It is a simple principle but a difficult task. As a matter of fact, most changes we need to make in life are simple, but that does not mean they are easy. Any change will take desire, hard work, discipline, consistency, and perseverance. You will have to fight some battles. You will hurt some feelings, and you may even lose some friends. Be prepared to be separated from some people for a while until consequences are enforced.

Don't ask God to guide your footsteps if you are not willing to move your feet!

Boundaries Questions
*Identify the rules that apply
within the framework of your life.*

Name one person you are uncomfortable being around and state why:

_____

_____

Identify one area in your life where boundaries are not properly controlled:

_____

_____

_____

_____

What one habit could you eliminate that would make a difference in your relationships?

_____

_____

_____

_____

What one habit could you establish in your life that would improve your relationships?

_____

_____

_____

_____

Budgeting
*Without a budget,
how do you know when you have enough?*
Anonymous

Money may be the most emotionally charged issue in life. For some, money is a god; for others, it is a security. Some use money as a tool to do well; others use it as a weapon to destroy. It can be a means to an end, or a source of freedom or power. **But money does not care how you use it.**

Most people fail to budget their money for three main reasons: fear of failure, fear of change, and fear of knowledge (what they will find out). Fear of failure is logical; the first attempts may very well fail. It typically takes about three months of budgeting to get it right. The fear of change is also logical; if you are not willing to change, you cannot succeed. But, the fear of knowledge is illogical. Knowledge will not change anything – and, anyway, you already know what you owe and what you make. You just have not taken the time to put the numbers on paper so you can control them.

Prosperity is not a specific amount of money. It is simply having your needs and desires met. To meet those needs, you must know where you stand with money, which means you need a budget. **Without a budget, how do you know when you have enough?**

Why Budget?

Now that we know why people do not budget, what are some of the reasons why they should?

- When you budget, you put yourself in control – not just of what you spend, but also what you keep;

- You reduce stress - No more worrying about whether you do or don't have what you need - now you know;
- Budgeting allows you to help yourself and to help others; and
- Budgeting allows you to set an example for those following (and watching) you.

When you spend money, someone else benefits, and so do you if the purchase was worthwhile. If you sell a car, the proceeds go in your pocket. If the car you sold is of value, the person purchasing it now has reliable transportation. When you have money and use it, you and the person you spend it with both have the value. Everyone wins. How you look at money will determine how you use it.

Our lives consist of four worlds: **Physical, mental, emotional,** and **spiritual**:

- Our **physical** world is where we need things.
- Our **mental** world is how we think about the things we need.
- Our **emotional** world is how we feel about those things.
- And our **spiritual** world is what we believe about them.

We are all programmed with a money blueprint. How you feel in your heart will dictate your behavior. A lack of money is never the problem. It is simply a symptom of what is going on at the roots. How can you help the poor if you are one of them? Your money blueprint comes from:

1) **education** regarding money,
2) **experience** with money,
3) **association** with wealth or poverty,
4) **memories** from youth, and
5) family **background**.

To change our perceptions, we must first become aware of them and study to understand them. If you want to go to the next level in life, you have to let go of some of the old ways of thinking. Knowledge allows change by disassociating ourselves with old ideas and reconditioning ourselves to new ones – it allows us to change habits. You can be a really nice person and be either rich or poor. But if you believe money is a bad thing, your mind will not allow you to accumulate it. **Resenting the rich is one of the surest ways to stay broke.** If no one in your family has ever been wealthy, break the mold so no other member of your family will ever be able to say that again. You can be the example to follow.

Money is a tool in that it allows you to obtain the things you need to go forward in life. It is like oil in that it makes life run more smoothly. Money is like a brick in that you can use it to build an outhouse or you can use it to build a cathedral. But my favorite analogy of money is that it is like manure: if you pile it up, it stinks, but if you spread it around, it helps things grow. It is how you use money that is the test of your character and your heart. When you pass the test of spending well, you become an example for others to follow.

Money can serve many purposes. It can provide good. You can send money where you do not have the ability or time to go: to build homes, adopt a child, or support a cause. Money can be used as a weapon (for good or evil). It can fight crime or support it. Money gives freedom from debt, provides stability, and reduces stress. Money gives power. The more you have the more you can bless and help others. How it is used determines its goodness or badness.

Many have been taught to believe you can't have a successful career and good, close relationships, or you can't focus on business and also have fun, or you can't have money and meaning in life. But you can; you do not have to choose between them. Get rid of the either/or thinking. When the nature of the person is pure, their actions will be pure regardless of the money. Wealth builders work hard, are productive and spend frugally. *"Most wealthy people are business owners who work hard and provide products and services that enhance and enrich our lives. The hard work ethic is essential to wealth building. . ."* **(Rich God, Poor God,** John Avanzini**)** Money, if you control it, makes a great servant; but, if you do not control it, it makes a lousy master. Knowing where you stand with it keeps it from controlling you. When what you do is a benefit to others, you deserve to be paid. Just because you prosper, does not mean someone else loses. (Luke 10:7)

The poverty mentality has a tendency to blame others, justify actions, and complain a lot. Poverty never encourages the highest level of the human spirit. Many believe wealth is wrong because of Matthew 19:23-24, where Jesus says, *"it is easier for a camel to go through the eye of the needle than for a rich man to enter Heaven."* He used this example because, in order for the camel to get through a small passageway, the camel has to take off its entire burden and be blindfolded so it does not get distracted by the challenge. For us to get to Heaven, we must do the same.

There are four basic ways people make money:

1. The majority of Americans make money through a job. They are an **employee** working for someone else being paid for the effort they give = work income

2. Another growing portion of the population makes money through **self-employment**. In effect, they own a job. They are still trading time for money but they have a little more control of the work they do = work income
3. **Owning a business** is where others work for you and you also get a portion of what they do = work income + passive income
4. **Investments** are the next way to bring in money. Investing is when you make money from the money you have already earned = investments

(If you want additional information in this area, Robert Kiyosaki wrote a book called **Rich Dad Poor Dad** that gives details on this subject.)

About 80% of Americans receive income through either a job or a small business. However, about 80% of earnings are in the area of business owners and investors, through passive income.

Budgeting is the best, most practical, way to keep track of your spending. To determine your net worth, this is the formula:

Net Worth = Income + Savings + Investments + Simplicity

- **Income** is the amount of money you bring in from work and passive income from prior work.
- **Savings** are the funds you save as you give up instant gratification and look at your future needs.
- **Investments** are those funds you collect from growing equity and stocks/bonds, etc.
- **Simplicity** is creating a lifestyle that requires you to spend less than you bring in.

In order to budget, you must know how much money you bring in each month, how much you plan to give away, and how much you want to save. For many faiths, according to God, 10% tithe is not an option. Ironically, most budgeting business professionals also recommend you give 10%. It has been proven that companies who give 10% are more successful than those who don't. You should also save 10%, even if it hurts, and live on the remaining 80%. This estimate will let you know how much you have to budget for your life expenses.

You then need to determine how much you are currently spending. The only way to know for sure what you are spending is to track the money every day for a month. Get a spiral book small enough to carry around with you or 3 x 5 cards and literally list every penny you spend. At the top of each page put the day of the week and the date. Then create four columns: one for **Time**, one for **Dollars**, one for **Item purchased**, and one for **Feeling** - write a one-word description of how you felt each time you spent money. This record will allow you to go back and see when you are spending, where you spent, and how you were feeling at the time you spent. For example, see below:

Date: _____   **Day of the Week:** _____

Time	Dollars	Item Purchased	Feeling
7:30	$ 1.06	Coffee	Tired

One thing I determined for myself when I did this exercise was that I spent more money on Tuesdays at noon than any other day or time of the week. I ate lunch out each Tuesday and, otherwise, I had a tendency to make my own lunch. With this knowledge, I could then decide if the lunch was worth the time, effort, and expense or not. This exercise allows you to see where you are spending frivolously and how your thoughts play a part in your spending. It makes it possible for you to target where you spend your money and to trim in areas that are not vital. The more knowledge you have before you start to budget, the easier it will be to create a budget you can live by.

It will not do you any good to create a budget unless you plan to follow it. Before you start the budget, set up a separate savings account and be sure to balance the checking and savings accounts each month. Know in advance what you are saving for and don't touch the funds in the savings account until you have accumulated the amount you planned or have reached the designated date or opportunity you planned to use the funds for.

Create goals for your money. One goal, if you have debt, will be to pay off bills. Here is how. List all of your bills in order of amount – smallest amount first. As you make the last payment on the smallest loan, add the amount you were paying on that bill to the payment of the next bill. These extra dollars will go toward the principle and pay the loan off much faster. If you have a debt with a high interest rate, do what you can to get the rate reduced. (If the amount of the bill is low enough to pay off in a reasonable time, you might want to put the higher interest rate bills higher on the list.)

Attached you will find an example of debt payoff. Four debt examples are given with a payoff in months. Round numbers are used just as an example. You will see in debt 1 that the last payment is only $10 (rather than the $30 in the prior months). The $20 savings can then be your bonus or reward for paying off the debt. The next month, the $30 you were paying on the first debt will be allocated to debt 2, making the payment on this debt now $130, rather than the previous $100 you were paying. Continue to do this until all bills are paid.

Do not create new debt while you are in this process. It is better to save for an item and pay in cash than to create debt which includes interest. (A home could be an exception to this rule.) Instant gratification is only rewarding for an instant. After that, it becomes a burden. From this point forward, do not create debt that cannot be paid off monthly.

Know the difference between your wants and your needs. Until you are out of debt, spend only on your needs. Even for your needs, shop for sales; however, do not buy just because something is on sale. Don't be an "impulse buyer."

Make budgeting a habit. It will change your life forever!

"... money is energy. Anxiety, stress and worry zap your energy and cut off your money flow." (Simon Bailey, *Shift your Brilliance: Harness the Power of You, INC.*).

A sample budget sheet is attached to help you determine what your monthly fixed expenses are. Then create another sheet just for you that includes all the bills you have accumulated and what you would need to pay on them each month to get them paid off. Call each lender, let them know your situation, and ask to negotiate a smaller amount or a lesser interest rate. Tell them how much you will be able to pay them each month and, whether they approve of the amount or not, pay it each month. Once you know where you stand, you can work on a solution to get you there.

Debt Example paid through accumulation

1	2	3	4
$100	$1,000	$2,000	$4,000
$30		$100	$100	$150
$30		$100	$100	$150
$30		$100	$100	$150
$10	**$20**	$100	$100	$150
		$130	$100	$150
		$130	$100	$150
		$130	$100	$150
		$130	$100	$150
		$80	**$50**	$100	$150
			$230	$150
			$230	$150
			$230	$150
			$230	$150
			$180	**$50**	$150
				$380
				$380
				$380
				$380
				$380

Highlighted amounts indicate funds you can spend as a reward for paying off the debt. The final $380 is now yours to spend. The next month put it in savings. For additional information on Budgeting, see www.daveramsey.com.

Quick Budget of
Monthly expenses to be paid

Food $_____

Housing $_____

Transportation $_____

Clothing $_____

Insurance $_____

Telephone $_____

Medicine/Medical bills $_____

Other $_____

$_____

$_____

$_____

$_____

Total for basics $_____

Changes that Heal
Thoughts from the book by Dr. Henry Cloud
*You can't change the circumstances, the Seasons, or the wind,
but you can change yourself.*
Jim Rohn

There is only one person responsible for the quality of your life; and if you turn that responsibility over to anyone else, you lose control. To be successful, you have to give up blaming and complaining. Because, if you admit you are in charge, then you can change things. Stop looking outside of yourself for the answers to why you are not where you want to be. George Washington Carver says: *99% of all failures come from people who have a habit of making excuses.*

When an event happens, your response will determine the outcome. Every outcome you experience in life is the result of how you have responded to an earlier event. If you are blaming and complaining, you cannot change the situation. The reason most people complain and blame is because they are afraid of the risk they have to take to change. But action overcomes fear.

The truth is the truth, whether you acknowledge it or not. Once you face it, you have an opportunity to change it. People almost always imagine the worst when they don't know what the truth is. You **CAN** change your thinking, change your communication, and change the pictures you allow in your head. You can change your image of yourself and change what you do. *"Change is the law of life. Those who look only to the past or present are certain to miss the future."* John F. Kennedy. You can change what you read, what you watch, how you talk to yourself, and whether you smile or not.

Don't be so controlled by your habits that you don't change your behavior. If you want to automatically go in a good direction, your habits have to take you there. Do more of what works; less of what doesn't work -- change your habits and try new behaviors to change the result. The only starting point that works is here and **NOW**, where you are.

Living a life of purpose means doing what you love to do and what you know you're good at; accomplishing what is important to you. Live your life on purpose. **Most people don't get what they want out of life because they don't know what they want out of life.** Success in life comes when you determine what you are committed to. It is not what life delivers that is important. It is what you do with your portion that is the determining factor. *"You weren't an accident. You weren't mass produced. You were deliberately planned, specifically gifted, and lovingly positioned on the earth by the Master Craftsman"* (Max Lucado). What we are is God's gift to us. What we become is our gift back to Him.

Focus on what you want from life, not what you don't want. If you want to be happy, focus on goals that command your thoughts and attention and inspire your hopes. As stated earlier, people only change when they hurt enough that they have to, they learn enough that they want to, and they believe enough that they are able to. Goals will take you outside your comfort zone. That's good, because outside your comfort zone is the only place you can grow. Use your imagination and develop some goals that drive you to enjoy life. *"Imagination is everything. It is the preview of life's coming attractions."* (Dr. Henry Cloud). If you imagine something clearly enough and work hard enough, you can achieve it. *"What the mind of man can conceive and believe, it can achieve"* (Napoleon Hill).

Hurt always interferes with clear thinking. The hurt of change is in the emotions. Passion and desire trump knowledge. People are more likely to change when they are shown a truth that influences their feelings than when given an analysis designed to shift their thinking. Psalm 73:21-22 says, *"When my heart was grieved and my spirit embittered, I was senseless and ignorant, I was a brute beast before You."* The problems we face today cannot be solved using the same methods that created them. If you keep doing what you have always done, you will keep getting what you already have. A good way to stretch your comfort zone is to bombard your mind with new thoughts and images. *"Those who cannot change their minds cannot change anything"* (George Bernard Shaw). The definition of insanity is doing what you have always done and expecting a different outcome. *"Many times we won't change until the pain of remaining the same is greater than the pain of change"* (Wayne Cordeiro).

We are responsible for our actions and our thoughts. We cannot go where we want to go in life if we do not take responsibility for our feelings and our actions. *"If you change the way you look at things, the things you look at change."* (Wayne Dyer). If we do something, something happens; if we do nothing, nothing happens. Our abilities are unique. That's why it is important to work in the area of our ability. We don't always think about what we are thinking about. We just let thoughts wander through our minds without direction or question.

Until we recognize and admit that things are not going as we would like them to, we have no reason to want to change. There are ten basic reasons why people fail to change:

1. **Poor people skills**. People don't listen, are not sensitive to others, or prefer to criticize, blame or complain.
2. **Negative attitude**. *"Two men looked from prison bars: one saw mud, the other stars."* When you learn to make the best of everything that happens, you remove a serious obstacle that stands in the way of change.
3. **Not working in an area of ability**. It is difficult to get excited about making a change if you are not changing in a direction that leads to enjoyment and self-fulfillment.
4. **Lack of focus**. No one can move forward without knowing where they want to go.
5. **Weak commitment**. Most people fail to change because they stop trying. And they stop trying because they do not recognize the benefit of the change.
6. **Unwillingness to change**. Some people are so in love with the past that they cannot deal with the present or see the future.
7. **Short-cut mindset**. Cutting corners is a sign of impatience, immaturity, and poor self-discipline.
8. **Relying on talent alone**. Adding a strong work ethic to talent is like pouring gas on a fire. It's explosive.
9. **Poor information**. You must know the changes you want to make and the steps you have to take to make them.
10. **No goals**. It is impossible to know when you succeed, if you do not know what you are aiming for.

Let go of your defenses and discover what weakens you, so you can start to do something about it. Most of our defenses are from the families we are raised in or the long-term relationships we live in. Defenses are necessary and important when you are in an unsafe environment, but you have to release them in safety if you want to change. Denial of an issue keeps you stuck in the problem. Often we deny because we don't want to want what we think we can't have, so we make something less valuable to us than it really is. Until our needs are met, our behavior will not change. *"Our dilemma is that we hate change and love it at the same time; what we really want is for things to remain the same while they get better"* (Sidney J. Harris). We don't want to have to change in order to change: we want the cancer to go away without the treatment; we want to get the job without going through the interview; and we want to be physically fit while we watch television. We want to have our cake and eat it too.

We cannot grow in a vacuum. **"People who need people are the luckiest people in the world."** Reach out to others even when it is uncomfortable. It is a first step toward positive change even though it opens you up for more hurt. We do not live in a pain-free world. You need new relationships to undo old learning. If you don't open the door to your heart, no one, including God, can come in. *"People who are crazy enough to think they can change the world are the ones who do"* (Rob Siltanen).

Here is a four-point plan for achievement: 1. Find a purpose; 2. Eliminate excuses; 3. Develop incentives; and 4. Cultivate determination.

To successfully change, you need a strategy. You have to create a sense of urgency. How fast do you want this change to happen? It is dangerous to change where you are until you know where you want to be. Take the time to create a vision and list the steps you have to take to create it. Then communicate the vision and find people to help you along the way. Determine the risk you have to take to create the vision of change that will make a difference in your life. When you have created the change you want, nurture it and make it a new habit.

As you pursue the necessities of life (health, food, shelter, money), don't forget the spirit and character you want to develop. What you become is far more important than what you do. Without a purpose you will stop at the first roadblock. Change is not easy; it is scary. Don't allow yourself to be content before you reach your goal. Reward yourself each step along the way. The only difference between a "big shot" and a "little shot" is the big shot kept on shooting. Holding on to something that you think is good for you now may be the reason you don't have something better. C. S. Lewis says, *"It may be hard for an egg to turn into a bird; it would be a jolly sight harder for it to learn to fly while remaining an egg . . . we must be hatched or go bad."*

"The best thing you can do is the right thing; the next best thing you can do is the wrong thing; the worst thing you can do is nothing."

Theodore Roosevelt

For change to happen, it must be planned. We all change at different rates and we only change if we believe in the vision of change. To change we have to recognize there is a need and understand the value of it. We have to put something in place to keep us from returning to old ways. It is your desire to change that will make it happen. If it is not a priority for you, you will not succeed. Change is almost always resisted and the only way to minimize the resistance is to thoroughly explain the need. Expect the unexpected. Be ready to make adjustments as needed. If there are no consequences to not changing, there will be greater resistance to change.

We do not fail at change because we are stupid. We fail because we have not yet experienced highly successful change, which means we have not created enough faith that the change will happen or will work. Thus, we do not try our hardest. With a healthy brain, you will never reach a point in life where you are incapable of learning new things.

It is only what you do after you get back up that counts.

Changes that Heal
Thoughts from the book by Dr. Henry Cloud

What is your area of ability?

_____

_____

_____

When you are healthy, what one additional change could you make that would change your life?

_____

_____

_____

What is the biggest stumbling block to you making this change?

_____

_____

_____

What reward will you give yourself when you have made this change?

_____

_____

_____

Choices

If you don't choose, someone else will choose for you!

Many years ago, I went to a Skip Ross seminar. Skip Ross is the author of "Say Yes to Your Potential." You can check him out at www.skipross.com. The first words out of his mouth were, *"You are right now exactly where you want to be in life."* I was absolutely convinced that was not true for me and I think there were several audience members who wanted to go on stage and choke him. You may feel the same way about me when I tell you, with confidence, *you are today exactly where you want to be in life.* Because, you see, we are where we are because of the choices we have made. And that is a good thing, because it means all we have to do to get a different outcome is to change the choices we make. Granted, many of the things that happen to us in life were not things we controlled, but what we do control is our reaction to the things that happen. How we choose to react is a determining factor in where we end up.

There are two sayings that come to mind – one from a friend, and the second from my son, Jason. I have a friend whose favorite quote is, *"It is what it is!"* Meaning, we can't change it (a little like the weather). I guess that means we need to work on the "isn'ts" that we might have some control over. The second quote is from my middle son, Jason. We were talking one day about a friend's accident and I said, "Jason, he could have died doing that." And Jason said, *"Mom, what didn't happen, can't!"* That's powerful. Think about all the things it could apply to:

If I had a different set of parents... If my friend had not betrayed me...

If the accident had not happened... If I had only known...

What didn't happen, can't! It is what it is! Any time spent thinking about these things is a total waste of energy. It is a choice. Hold on to the negative thoughts, pain, hurt, and embarrassment, or let them go.

Most of what we will discuss is not new. You've heard it before. There may even be some points we discuss that you will later realize, "So-in-so has been telling me that for years." But because you hear it from another source – someone who cannot possibly be criticizing you (because I don't even know you well enough to be critical) – you will hear it. As a matter of fact, at least one of you will read something in this article, go home and explain it to someone else, and they will say to you (or at least think it) *"That is exactly what I have been saying"*. You did not hear it because you felt it was criticism rather than advice. Understand, if I did personally criticize you, I would be the biggest hypocrite in the room. The only reason I can teach you is because I have done everything wrong at least once. I've held on to pain, hurt, and embarrassment to the detriment of myself and my children and others. I have failed to set goals and failed to reach them (and still do). So, what you will get from me is experience not perfection.

Because I love the Lord, I always assume that the number one reason we were created was to properly represent Him. This chapter is designed to help us determine how to best do this through work and lifestyle. What specific talents do we have in us individually that will help us fulfill that purpose? Charles Stanley defines success as *"...the continuing achievement of becoming the person God wants you to be and accomplishing the goals God has helped you to set... Our success always has conditions on it and the conditions are primarily spiritual."*

We are going to do a lot of work in this topic. If you take it seriously, when you complete the work you will have the knowledge you need to change your tomorrow. If you do this year what you did last year, you will have next year what you have now. Nothing will seriously change. We were created with the ability to make choices, but we fail to recognize what a serious blessing that is, or how POWERFUL making a choice can be.

John Maxwell says if you choose to spend one hour a day every day studying and working on any particular thing, in five years you will be an expert at it. You could learn a foreign language; become an airline pilot; win a tennis tournament; be a better parent, spouse, friend. You cannot develop a relationship with anyone without time. So, how would your relationships improve if you spent one hour a day every day developing them? There are no limits to what you can do or be if you make the right choices.

Everything we do is a choice – even not selecting an alternative is making the choice not to choose. Even in the worst possible situation, we have a choice. Victor Frankel chose not to give in or give up in the German concentration camp – even after losing his entire family. He had no control over what happened to his family, but he had a purpose and a mission to help others survive. There is also a purpose and a mission for your life. You have talents you can use to help others and you can choose what you want to be remembered for.

Ask any six-year-old what they want to be in life, and they "light up like a candle" with all their ideas. My "stolen" granddaughter wanted to be a firefighter, a ballerina, and a dentist. Her mother is a firefighter, and every little girl want to be a ballerina – but we don't know where the dentist came from.

When we are children, our dream circle is huge. When we become adults and start to make a living, our income circle is much smaller than our dream circle - after years of living, things change. In order for us to maintain sanity, one of two things have to happen. We either have to decrease our dreams or increase our income.

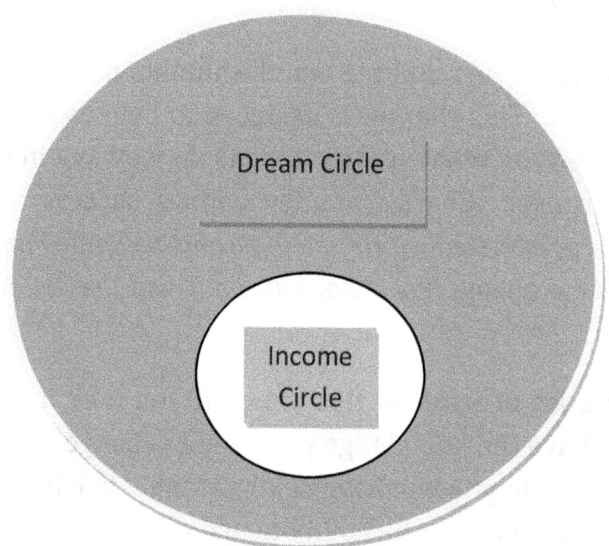

Most Americans reduce their dreams <u>and</u> then increase their income through the use of credit cards. According to American Consumer Credit Counseling (2016), the U.S. credit card debt in the United States is, on average, over $5,700 per adult. Households with the lowest net worth hold an average of over $10,000 in credit card debt.

Actually, though it seems like a contradiction, the best solution to the problem of income versus dreams circles is to increase the dreams. Having big dreams forces you to get outside of your comfort zone (and you cannot grow inside your comfort zone). Remember, every other thing you want – everything you want that you don't have right now – is outside of your comfort zone.

For some of you, "dreaming" is childish. If that's the case, change the word "dreaming" to "visualizing." Both words mean to see in your mind's eye what you would like to see, whether it is true or not.

Try an exercise: Close your eyes. Visualize an elephant. What is the elephant doing? Walking through the woods? Fighting? Drinking from the water hole? Tending the babies? Where is the elephant -- in the zoo or on the plains of Africa? Most will see a grey elephant. MAKE YOUR ELEPHANT PINK! If you did not have any trouble seeing a pink elephant, you just proved to yourself that you have the ability to visualize (or dream). Now, let's use that ability.

Now that we understand the process, let's learn to break down the goals into categories that will lead to the ultimate goals for your life. We spend a lot of time imagining things. Let it be things we want to have happen. When God gives you a vision, He also gives you the ability to get it done. Think and choose today so you don't have to regret tomorrow.

When you have done anything once, the second time is easier. The first time you cook a meal, change a tire, or drive to an unknown location, all these things are challenging. However, once you have done it, no matter how long it took or how confusing it may have been, you know you can do it again. That event is now in your comfort zone. Oops! Now you have to come up with something else to do that you have not done, so you can keep growing.

Very few people take the time to determine what they want their lives to look like. Even fewer put the plans they do have in writing. You now have the ability to choose to be a part of the minority! Over and over it has been proven that people who write down their dreams and break them down into bite-size pieces are the people who actually accomplish what they want to accomplish in their lives. Knowing what you want is essential. Doing what you need to do is critical.

Writing down goals makes it more likely that they will actually be achieved. It's a choice. Will you write them down or not? God has no objection to any goal we set that will help us (or someone else) to draw closer to Him. Think, talk, act, and dress as if you were already the person you want to be. Study people who are doing what you want to do and emulate them. Make choices that take you where you want to go.

- Choose different friends. Be with people who are going where you want to go.
- Improve your work ethic; be more timely, more reliable, and more productive.
- Study to improve yourself and practice what you learn.
- Start an exercise program – even if all you can do is chair exercises, do something.

- Choose a healthy diet, eat more regular meals, and control your portions.
- Choose to go to bed at the same time every night and get up at the same time every morning so your body gets regulated for good sleep.
- Choose to spend your time wisely.
- Get organized.
- Improve your language skills.

You can choose to love, forgive, serve, and stand. But it does not happen automatically. It is a choice you make. As soon as you choose to pay the price for your dreams, you will reap the benefits for the rest of your life. Change your "would've" "should've", "could've" to **WILL**. When we die, God will not be nearly as pleased with what we did as with what we did that He asked us to do. A good life is not a lucky thing some people stumble into, but rather a wonderful thing responsible people choose and create!

Choices

What do you like to do?

_____

_____

What do you do well? (List at least three things)

_____   _____

_____   _____

As a child, what did you want to be when you grew up?

_____

_____

What do you feel is your strongest talent?

_____

_____

What do other people say you are good at?

_____

_____

What do you see yourself doing in five years?

Where would you live? _____

Where would your parents live? _____

What kind of car would you drive? _____

Where would your children (grandchildren) go to school? _____

Would you continue your education? _____ Where? _____

What would you study? _____

Where would you go on vacation? _____

What charity or church would you support? _____

How would you support them? Mission? Money? _____

Who else would you help? _____ How? _____

What kind of work would you do? _____

What do you want to be remembered for? _____

_____

_____

_____

_____

Communication
Saying what you mean in a way that others understand

Man is the only creature with the ability to speak. What a privilege! Not only do we have the same ways of communicating as all animals, we also have the ability to express what we think and feel with words. Words, properly used, are priceless. *"A word fitly spoken is like apples of gold in pictures of silver."* (Proverbs 25:11)

All other created beings are born with knowledge that shows them how to survive: how to get food and protect their young, and themselves even how to communicate within their species:

- Wild animals like the wolf teach their young how to fight as a unit to defend or capture.
- When geese fly south, they go in formation and switch positions to give the leader rest.
- When an eagle has eaglets in the nest, she will sit on them and pull them under her wings when it rains so they don't get wet.
- When an elephant trumpets, it is heard for miles and brings the family members together.
- Ants and bees build huge homes to protect their queen, working together as an army.

Man is given all that wisdom and, on top of that, the ability to think, plan, love, and worship. No other creature has this ability. With that ability comes responsibility. Speech is a wonderful gift, but it is also a complicated gift. Interpreting what is said has not only to do with the language used, but also with the receiver's understanding of what the words mean. Even if both parties speak the same language, the definition of the words spoken often varies with the age, life experience, and education of the one spoken to.

Inappropriate language makes us look uneducated, often makes the other person feel threatened, and reflects poorly on character. It is counter-productive and even dangerous. If we plan to advance in relationships or careers, it is important to show respect to others, and profanity is perceived as disrespectful. But it is not just inappropriate language, and this is a problem.

Improper language is also a challenge, primarily because it is so common to the one using it that it is not seen as a problem. Most of the time, poor English is simply a matter of bad habit or a lack of education – which means it can be corrected with effort. For example: When a person says, "I seen," that is poor English. The phrase is either "I saw" or "I have seen." That is simply a matter of learning the English tenses of past, present, and future. This is especially common among speakers where English is a second language.

When every other word out of the mouth is "like", "um", "ah" or "you know", this is usually a sign of discomfort – or, again, bad habit. It is distracting from the communication, which sometimes keeps the listener from hearing what is being said.

These problems, though common, are not necessarily easy to fix, because changing habits and studying take time, effort, and self-discipline. And, if the only conversations are among peers or the common, "How are you," change may not be necessary. But if you are in a job interview, or building a business with clients, or attempting to address the public, good communication is critical.

Talking and communicating are not the same thing. All too often, when someone else is speaking, the person who is supposed to be listening is actually formulating what they want to say, and they miss the point being made. Equally as often, the person speaking has failed to communicate significant and substantial information, because they did not take the time to evaluate what they were saying before they spoke. If done correctly, communication includes two talents – speaking and listening. Please note that speaking and listening are learned traits.

Communication Process

The process of communication includes the sender, the message, and the receiver. First, the sender has an idea to be related. The idea is then communicated (encoded) by words or symbols (through filters) to the receiver. The receiver then translates (or decodes) the information sent: Idea ⟶ Encoded ⟶ Decoded

If the receiver receives the same information the sender sends, communication has taken place. Unfortunately, many times, this is not the case. For communication to take place, you must have an effective speaker, a common understanding of the barriers in the way, and an active listener.

Effective Speaking

Effective communication occurs only if the receiver understands the exact information or idea that the sender intends to transmit. Words used only account for 7% of what is perceived; voice tone counts for 38%; and facial expressions counts for 55%. As you can see, the last two (voice and facial expressions) make up 93% of communication (Fenson, 2000). So, don't send conflicting messages by nodding "yes" while you are saying or thinking "no." Unless facial expressions, body language, and eye contact agree with what is being said, little understanding is achieved.

When you have an important issue or idea to express, take the time to think before you speak. To insure effective and efficient communication, know in advance the purpose for the communication. It is difficult to make your message understood if you are not sure what your message is yourself. Establish an aim, plan what you say, and check to be sure you have been understood. Give as much information as needed and leave out unnecessary details.

If your audience is American, make eye contact with your listener. Here, eye contact conveys interest, concern, and warmth. If, however, you are in another culture, know the rules. In many Asian countries, eye contact is a sign of disrespect or aggression. Often, before a word is even spoken a feeling is conveyed -- emotions radiate. Joy may cause excitement and anger can cause stress. Good posture and body language signal confidence. Different cultures, life experiences, and perceptions – as well as education and health – often contribute to misunderstandings.

When you are speaking, ask the listener if they are following you. Use words that the listener is likely to understand. Do not ignore signs of confusion. Make listening easier by varying your voice tones and using your body gestures and facial expressions to relay the same message you are speaking. **SMILE** frequently.

Show **M**ore **I**nterest and **L**ess **E**go.
(It's not just about you!)

Communication Barriers

Focus on the other person's feelings. The words spoken mean what the speaker thinks they mean – not what the dictionary says they should mean. Because of different **cultures**, **life experiences**, and **perceptions**, we often misunderstand what is being said by allowing our past experiences to change the meaning of the message. We have a tendency to focus on ourselves rather than the speaker, which leads to defensiveness (we feel someone is attacking us), superiority (we feel we know more than the speaker knows), and ego (we feel we are, or should be, the center of the activity).

We can also be distracted by **outside noise** (either conversations going on around us, machinery, traffic, or radios), bright lights, an attractive person (or someone we know), unusual sights, or many other stimuli.

Stress is an additional barrier to communication. People do not see things the same way when they are under stress. What we see, hear, or believe can be altered by our frame of mind.

Another major barrier to communication is **personal feeling** toward the speaker or the listener. Whether positive or negative, we often perceive the message in the vein we expect it to be delivered. Listen first before you try to evaluate what the speaker is trying to say and judge the information rather than the speaker.

Barriers are much like filters. The message leaves the speaker, goes through the filters (the listener's mind), and is then heard by the receiver. The only way to process through the filters is to listen actively.

Active Listening

Most people speak at 100 to 175 words per minute, but they can intelligently listen at 600 to 800 words per minute. You can see how the "80/20 rule" would apply here. Since we have the ability to think and listen at the same time, we only actively receive about 20% of all we hear – unless we put some techniques in place to increase our ability to listen. Therefore, without forcing ourselves to focus, only part of our mind is on what is being said. In order to stay focused, you have to listen with a purpose. Without true listening, good communication is not possible. Listening is an active process and requires focus. It is the foundation of understanding another person and no other communication techniques will be of value until that foundation is solid.

Listening is the act of hearing sounds and decoding them into meanings. It takes as much energy (if not more) to listen as it does to speak. Some aids to active listening would include:

- Look the speaker in the eye.
- Ask a question when something is unclear.
- Rephrase what the speaker says to be sure you understand.
- Don't jump to conclusions or formulate your response until the speaker finishes speaking.
- Don't change the subject or become preoccupied with your own thoughts.
- Take notes.

Many things can distract us from listening and one of the most common is feeling the information we are receiving does not apply to us. Many good ideas are missed by not paying close enough attention. If you find yourself in a meeting where you cannot leave, listen hard for the one sentence that could make a difference to you.

Follow-up

Before the participants end the communication, they should take the time to give each other feedback on what they understood from the transaction. Communication is a give and take, an exchange of ideas, as all parties must participate to complete the information exchange. To summarize, to insure effective and efficient communication:

- Know in advance the reason for the communication and what outcome you want to achieve.
- Understand the message sent to you.
- Learn to listen before you speak.
- Words mean what the speaker intends not what the dictionary records.
- Look for and clarify ambiguities.
- Correct any inconsistencies.

- Rephrase what the speaker has said.
- For any meetings you are involved in, write down your understanding and, when appropriate, distribute it to others involved.
- Give the other person an opportunity to finish what they are saying before you speak.

Communication Tips

For ongoing communication:
- Give as much information as possible up front.
- Have brief, regular updates.
- Pass along any changes quickly.
- Ask open-ended questions (not just "yes" and "no" answers).
- Document the conversation.
- Be open to others' perspectives.

Forms of Communication

No technical device has ever improved on **face-to-face** contact with another person. "Face" time is crucial. New technology has made communication so much more convenient, but, to some extent, it has robbed us of the opportunity to truly know each other. When we communicate through any method other than face-to-face, we can miss the facial expressions, body language, and voice tones which make up 93% of the communication. Even Skype and Zoom do not allow you to feel the emotions of the one you are speaking with. So, whatever methods you use, be sure to include face-to-face communication as often as possible.

Communication through **meetings** follows a similar procedure: plan beforehand for the number of people to attend, the purpose of the meeting, the time, duration, agenda, and information needed in advance, as well as the location. Monitor during the meeting to be sure you don't get sidetracked and then review afterwards to be sure all understood the same message. This is especially important if you are communicating with someone from another culture, language, or background.

Personal, **handwritten notes** are the next most personal form of communication. Keep note cards handy to send off a quick "thank you" or "good job" message. Pre-stamp and return addressed blank cards and keep a couple in your planner so you can send off a message immediately when you have a meeting with a potential client or employee.

When you are using the **telephone**, the receiver does get the voice tone (though not the facial expressions), but it is often difficult to reach the receiver with the schedules most people keep today. So, that leaves us with electronic devices.

When you are communicating through **electronic devices** (especially with people you are not familiar with), remember that your message must be much clearer as the receiver cannot see your body or facial expressions nor hear your voice tones. Words spoken with a smile can come across as harsh on paper.

Good communication saves time and energy. When you make your point quickly, you can go on to other things.

Remember: You never get a second chance at a first impression!

Remember, when someone slaps you verbally, you have the choice to turn the other cheek, flee, grovel, or hit back. If your choice is to hit back, your opponent now has those same choices. Much of our pain has its source not in our faith or our values, not in our weakness or our strength, but in our language. "Sticks and stones may break my bones, but words will never harm me" is a totally false statement.

To understand what another person is saying, we must assume that what they are saying is true (at least from their perspective). Hearing what is said with a closed mind prevents you from understanding or helping the other person.

For communication to be successful, it must end with peace on both sides, with each person feeling that they have been heard, and with a great desire to continue developing the relationship.

Communication

Take notes when you are listening to the news and see how much more you remember.

_____

_____

_____

What do you find to be your main distractions when you try to listen? Make a list of the top three distractions and next time you are in a conversation be aware of them.

_____

_____

_____

Pay attention to your body language. When you are thinking hard, do you have a furrowed brow, which makes you look angry? What are some ways you could change the way you stand, or hold your hands, or use your facial expressions that would make a conversation go more in your favor?

_____

_____

_____

Conflict Resolution

Conflict is an **external event** between two or more persons.

Conflict occurs because no two people are alike. We have different goals and values; we are interested in different things; and we have different needs and wants. As a result, we don't always agree with one another. Any time a choice is to be made there is potential for conflict because disharmony is felt by one party. Conflict means someone perceives a threat to their peace, and it will not go away until it is addressed – either with the other entities or within one's self.

Even though conflict can lead to anger, it is not the same as anger. Anger is an **internal emotion** letting you know that a want or need has been violated. It is a valuable God-given emotion that must be controlled when you are handling conflict. No one can make you angry. That is a decision you make for yourself.

For there to be a conflict, there has to be a disagreement on something. People who are depending on each other are disappointed because everyone cannot have all that they want; or resources are limited and often we feel the other person is a stumbling block for us. To solve a conflict, you have to recognize and state the source.

Often God puts us in conflicting positions to teach us humility, trust, or acceptance; or to motivate us to use the talents He has given us. Either way, conflict is not comfortable. When our conflict is with our Higher Power, we are in an excellent position in that we automatically know –whether we like it or not – He is right! In that case, we need to submit. However, most conflicts are with other people. Conflicts are often a result of personality traits: one person talks a lot and the other is withdrawn; one is an active doer and the other is more laid back. A good example of conflict as a result of different needs is in the parent/child relationship, where the child wants freedom and the parent has a need to protect and train.

There are several ways we can solve conflict. We can negotiate, moderate, arbitrate, or sue. The best way, if possible, is to negotiate. God says to esteem others greater than ourselves (Philippians 2:3). But He also says to love others as we love ourselves (Matthew 22:39). If we truly love others as ourselves, we will have a desire to also esteem them. It is important to know both sides of an issue (not just ours) if we are going to be able to solve a problem.

Conflict happens when needs are not met. So, let's look at the primary needs of basic personalities. The choleric personality needs **respect**, the melancholy needs **space**, the phlegmatic needs **security**, and the sanguine needs **attention**. It is important to know these needs when negotiating conflicting situations. (See the chapter on Personality Traits)

To get respect, the active doer must control their emotions (especially anger); the thinker must open lines of communication; the peacemaker must take on responsibility; and the excited one must listen actively. Again, not any of these actions are comfortable for that personality. For sure, anger, withdrawal, procrastination, and blaming – the typical reactions to conflict - do not work to solve conflict.

Conflict is stressful and stress interferes with the resolution. Stress keeps us from reading another person's emotions or even hearing what they are saying. It is important to keep emotions under control in order to communicate needs clearly.

Conflict is not necessarily bad. It brings differences to the surface where they can be addressed and resolved; and when they are resolved, they often enhance the understanding between the parties and improve the overall relationship.

People respond to conflict based on life experiences. A person who has been through abuse or abandonment will sometimes overreact to even a minor infraction, as if it were the end of a relationship. A person who has been over-protected may find it difficult to defend themselves. A person who has always gotten their way will find it hard to compromise. Once we close our minds, for whatever reason, communication becomes difficult; and without communication, resolution is not possible.

Learning to handle conflict may be one of the most important skills one needs to develop. Conflict resolution requires patience, which may mean letting the other person voice their needs first. If you first listen to what the other person feels is the problem, you are in a better position to handle and address their complaints and to determine if your complaints are valid. Listen before you speak. Don't think about what you are going to say until after you have heard what they have to say. Listen for what is felt as well as what is said. Listen without interrupting, with your head and your heart.

When it is your turn to express your thoughts, do so without blaming. Don't make assumptions; ask questions. Don't expect others to know your feelings if you have not communicated them. Know, understand, and control your own emotions. **You don't have to be friends, but you do need to be friendly.** Attack the problem not the person. Don't involve outsiders in the conflict unless it is absolutely necessary for the resolution. If you do need help, it is best to get a neutral party or a professional.

If time is available, the best method of solution is to work for a **win-win**. However, being realistic, collaboration is not always possible. In most cases, everyone has to give up something and some challenges will still exist. When a quick decision is mandatory, or a moral issue is involved, others' opinions may have to be set aside. This being the case, the relationship may be at risk. If nothing else works, you may simply have to use your authority to choose your own solution and come back later to smooth over hurt feelings or misunderstandings.

With some conflicts, the issue may not be important enough for you to work to get what you want. It may be more beneficial to the relationship to **accommodate** the other person's needs and create a "they win/I lose" scenario. All issues need to be addressed, but there are times when it is best to ignore the issue until more information is available or more time is available to address it. Ignoring an issue may be the best solution if neither of the parties feel the issue is important enough to address. Even though the issue will come up again, if it is not interfering or causing too much tension, it may be best to hold off on addressing it – no one wins and no one loses.

Most of the time the only solution to a conflict is to **compromise** – everyone has to give up something. You simply agree to disagree – everyone bends.

The method you use to negotiate through a conflict will depend on how much time you have, how much pressure you are under to make a decision, how important the issue is, and how much control you have in the decision; as well as what relationships exist between the parties.

Before you attempt to resolve a conflict, get your own emotions under control so you have the ability to listen and communicate well. Communicate with your heart and your ears before you involve your mouth. Keep your voice under control. Speak softly and stay friendly. Be sure your body language matches your words. **Be motivated to resolve the conflict, not just to win.**

Resolution Options

Most conflicts can be resolved through **negotiation** – each person expressing their needs and working together to get those needs met, which usually ends up with a win-win situation.

If, however, negotiation is not working, it may be necessary to bring in an outside person, a **mediator**. A Mediator can look at both sides objectively without bias and assist in coming to a conclusion where both sides compromise. The ultimate decision is made by the parties involved. The Mediator simply helps each side see the other side.

If mediation does not work, it may be necessary to go the next step to **arbitration**, where the outsider listens to both sides and actually comes up with the solution, and the decision is binding on both parties. This almost always ends up with one or more parties not being happy with the result.

Obviously, if none of these methods work, the courts may have to intervene. **Litigation** is the final step for conflict. It is an expensive step and a binding step and often leads to bitterness for one or all parties. It is to be avoided if at all possible. *"Settle matters quickly with your adversary who is taking you to court. Do it while you are still together on the way, or your adversary may hand you over to the judge, and the judge may hand you over to the officer, and you may be thrown into prison."* (Matthew 5:25)

Resolution Tips

To resolve an issue, you have to be as concerned for others as you are for yourself. Collaboration, where both parties' feelings and concerns are addressed, will lead to a win-win situation. Avoidance or denial of a problem will not resolve the problem. It will lead to stress and even physical illness, often making things worse. At the same time, yielding to the other person without regard for self can lead to bitterness.

Conflict is not always bad. It is far more common with people we know than people we do not. But solving conflict often leads to a more solid and fulfilling relationship in the end. It can serve as a catalyst for needed changes and an opportunity for personal growth through love, grace, and forgiveness. It is for this reason that it is so important to learn how to reconcile conflict with the least amount of aggression and the most amount of understanding.

Matthew 5:23-24 (NIV) *"Therefore, if you are offering your gift at the altar and there remember that your brother or sister has something against you, leave your gift there in front of the altar. First go and be reconciled to them; then come and offer your gift."*

Conflict Resolution

What are the basic strengths of your personality?

_____
_____
_____

What are your basic weaknesses?

_____
_____
_____

List three things that you know trigger conflict in you?

1. _____

2. _____

3. _____

If you could, how would you change the way you have handled conflict in the past? List three situations and state your changes.

_____
_____
_____
_____
_____

Credit Repair
The best tool to repair credit, and the best tool to prevent bad credit is a BUDGET!

All credit information is regulated by the Federal Trade Commission (FTC); but each state regulates the statute of limitations for collections. In the state of Michigan, the debtor is given 6 years (after the first missed payment) to collect an *unsecured* debt. (Check your state to see what rules apply.) After that, the debt cannot be legally pursued. Secured debts are usually settled by collecting the item or items that secure the debt.

Credit scores range from 300 to 850. A "good" credit score is considered 700 to 740. Credit scores are calculated in five different areas:

- ***Payment History*** accounts for 35% of your score – Do you pay on time?
- ***Credit utilization*** accounts for 30% of your score – How much debt do you have?
- ***Length of credit history*** accounts for 15% of your score –How long have you had each debt?
- ***Types of credit*** accounts for 10% of your score – Variety of accounts (loans, department stores, credit cards, etc.)
- ***Credit inquiries*** accounts for the last 10% of your score – How many inquiries have you had on your account?

Know where you stand! Bad credit is usually a result of no budget, poor budgeting, or not following the budget; which results in impulse buying – buying what you don't need when you can't afford to buy it – and not being able to keep up with the payments after the purchase. For you to determine where you stand, you need to acquire a copy of your credit report from one or all three credit-reporting agencies.

- Experian Agency: 1-888-397-3742 (www.experian.com)
- TransUnion Agency: 1-800-916-8800 (www.transunion.com)
- Equifax Agency: 1-800-685-1111 (www.equifac.com)

Due to human error or intent, many credit reports have inaccurate information on them.

Identify any misinformation. No one can legally remove accurate and timely negative information from a credit report. There is no quick fix for credit repair. However, incorrect information can be removed and you can do it yourself without paying a credit repair company. It will take persistence, tenacity, self-discipline, and determination (PTSD – which you have). It is not an easy process. To correct any errors you must first get a copy of your credit card. To get a free copy, call the Annual Credit Report agency at 1-877-322-8228 or go to www.AnnualCreditReport.com. You can do this once a year; or you can request a report from just one agency and in four months repeat the request for another, which gives you a credit report every four months. When you get your credit report, it will come with an *Investigation Form* for you to report any discrepancies. If there are errors, return the form Certified Mail and keep a copy for your records. The credit company then has 30 days to make the corrections. Include any documentation you have to prove your point.

When checking your report, watch the dates. Negative information stays on your report for 7 years (with the exception of Bankruptcy 13 and Bankruptcy 7 which stay on for 10 years). After the seven years, the listing should drop off automatically. If not, you need to address the issue.

Removing incorrect information from your credit report: Incorrect information on your credit report can come from many different sources. Stolen identity is a major problem in today's world and is very difficult to correct or repair. It typically requires court action. It is reported that the most common identity theft comes from a family member using your social security number to set up accounts. To report identity theft, go to www.identitytheft.gov for a recovery plan.

However, banks make errors in reporting and so do vendors. And, once they report a debt to be collected, they often forget to remove it when it is paid in full. It is your responsibility to monitor your credit report for these errors.

Some actions you can take to correct errors include:

- Place a fraud alert with each company that says you owe when you do not.
- Put a freeze on your Credit Report, so no one (including you) can apply for additional credit.

- Report the error to the Federal Trade Commission
- Write a letter to each company you do not owe with detail about the error and include any information you have that proves you are working to correct it. (Keep a copy)
- Write a letter to each vendor who had sent in incorrect information. (Keep a copy)
- Follow up in 30 days to see that the incorrect information has been removed.

Clearing real debt.

When you owe and are not able to pay, the bill may stay with the original debtor or it may be sold to a collection agency. If it is sold to a collection agency, you no longer owe the original debtor; you owe the agency, and all correspondence will go through them. Be sure to only communicate with them through a paper trail of letters or e-mails. **Do not negotiate with them on the phone.** They are notoriously known for not keeping records, so that in the future, if the bill comes up again, they will not verify that it has been paid. They have also been known to negotiate with you to pay a portion and then selling the rest of what is owed to another agency. So be sure that you have all communication in writing.

When you have cleared a debt, have the company or agency completely remove the item from the credit report – Not just document it as paid, but taken off completely. (This may have to be done by the original debtor rather than the agency; but they can do it for you.)

When paying off an old debt, pay with a cashier's check or money order and not with a personal check. Do not give your banking information out to a collection agency. You may even want to get the money order from a bank other than you own.

Steps you can take going forward:

God gave us a lot of valuable information on how to handle money and most of it is found in the book of Proverbs. Tithe is a necessity if you want God's blessing on your finances. But He also promises to take care of you if you follow His lead: *"Honor the Lord with thy substance, and with the first-fruits (tithe) of all thine increase: So shall thy barns be filled with plenty, and thy presses shall burst out with new wine."* (Proverbs 3:9-10)

Create a Budget. Having a budget you live by will stop the bleeding and, over time, increase your credit score. Budgeting is not easy, but it is mandatory if you want to get a handle on your money. It will help you pay your monthly bills on time.

While you are working to create and live by a budget, do not apply for any additional credit and come up with a plan to pay off the debts you do have. No impulse buying. Be frugal until you have your payments under control.

Creating a budget is simply a matter of adding and subtracting. No great math abilities are required. To create a budget you need to know how much you have coming in each month. When you determine your monthly income, you simply identify how much you give each month, how much you save each month, how much you owe in bills each month, and how much miscellaneous spending you do. Then you subtract the total expenses from the total income, and you will know where you stand with your money and where you need to make adjustments. This will require making a list of your monthly bills and tracking your daily spending to locate any discretionary income. It may require creating additional income to cover the expense if you are not currently bringing in enough.

Pay on time from now on. Paying on time is what scores the highest on your credit report (35%). Arrange your life to live within your means while you work to increase your income. Once you have a budget in place and you have eliminated debts, create a habit of paying monthly bills on time. Keep payment dates in your calendar so you are not late. Pay early when possible. Once you have a history of paying your utilities on time, **Experian Boost** is a free service that, on average, increases your score by 13 points because they are able to get your utility payments to count toward your Payment History.

Eliminate credit cards. Pay off the cards you have and do not apply for additional credit. A Debit Card will suffice for any purchase and will not allow you to spend what you do not have. If it is necessary to have a business credit card, be sure it is paid on a timely basis in full (not just minimum payments).

No impulse buying. Before you make a purchase, determine how it will affect your budget. Is it in your budget? How will you use it, when will you use it, and can you do without it? Don't make the purchase until you know it is of value and you can pay for it in a timely manner.

Create a Savings Account. Decide before you receive any income how much of it you are going to give away and how much of it you are going to save. Make it a goal to create a separate savings account that will take you through six months should any emergency happen. Don't spend it, don't touch it, don't think about it unless the emergency happens.

Be responsible. Set an example for those behind you to follow. When you make a purchase, you owe the vendor. To not pay puts them in a bad position. If you know you owe someone, work on putting the funds aside to pay. If they are not trying to collect from you, say nothing until you can pay and then pay in full. (Unfortunately, if they are not trying to collect and you make a partial payment, they can then come back and collect even if the six years for collection are up.) Do the right thing but be wise about it.

Credit Repair Questions

What expenses could you eliminate from your spending that would help you pay off your debts? What discretionary income do you have?

_____

_____

_____

_____

What could you do to create additional income?

_____

_____

_____

_____

What actions are you willing to take to improve your credit?

_____

_____

_____

_____

Decision-Making/Problem-Solving Process

"The world cares very little about what a man or woman knows;
it is what a man or woman is able to do that counts."
Booker T. Washington

Decision making is the mental process resulting in the selection of a course of action among several alternative scenarios. Small decisions shape the large decisions. Our decision making is limited by information, time, and mental ability and is the process of identifying problems and opportunities, developing alternative solutions, choosing a preferred alternative, and then implementing it.

You know you have a decision to make when you identify a problem or a need that has to be resolved. Problem-solving occurs when there is a need to move from one given state to a desired goal. When you are trying to solve a problem, it is imperative that you know what outcome you want to achieve before you decide what method you will use to solve the situation. Most problems are created from bad habits; bad habits which are usually automatic and come from our human nature of acting before we think. They are usually formed more quickly than good and take conscious recognition to resolve or change.

We face problems every day: need directions, car won't start, pen won't write, we break a shoelace or a fingernail. These are the little things. We don't always control their happening, but we always control how we react to their happening. Most of these challenges are small and easily resolved with a little effort. But, sometimes, we come across situations that take time, effort, and patience; like when we see an opportunity or recognize a threat. A threat refers to a current condition that is not desired or preferred; an opportunity is a chance for progress if a good decision is made.

Sometimes the decision you have to make is not between good and bad, but between better and best: between two good alternatives. To make a decision, you need wisdom. Don't be afraid to make a decision. The worst decision you can make is to not make one. Even a bad decision can be reversed. It may cost time and sometimes money, but few decisions are really fatal.

In order to create an environment for effective decision making, you have to provide time to collect information, form alternatives, and evaluate your opinions. There is an old Turkish proverb that says, "The devil interferes with fast work." In other words, if you don't take the time to do it right, it will be wrong. Keep your eyes open; disasters and accidents result from ignoring warning signs.

Skip Ross, author of *Say YES to your Potential*, said in one of his conferences: *"There are no problems. If a problem has a solution, it is not a problem; it is a fact of life. If a problem has a solution, it is still not a problem; it is a challenge. It has a solution. Determine the solution and then work on the solution and don't' think of the 'problem' again."*

Some research indicates there are **7 Cs of Decision Making**: There is no order to the 7 Cs. You must use all to make a good decision.

1. **Communication:** Clearly define the challenge so you have a chance of relating it to others so they can have input and help you with a decision
2. **Conviction:** Determine how important it is to make a decision on the issue. If it is important, be ready to stand up for what is right.
3. **Common Sense:** Common sense is not common. It is simply what you have learned from life experiences that work, and this can be dangerous. If your temper or emotions have gotten you what you want in the past, you may be led to believe using your temper is common sense.
4. **Compositions:** What are you made of? What are your talents? Each person has received gifts to be used to serve others.
5. **Counsel**: Choose your mentors wisely. Talk to others with experience in the areas you are working in.
6. **Circumstances:** Nothing happens by chance. Incidences in our life nudge us forward in different directions. However, be careful not to just go on circumstances. Remember the other 6 Cs.
7. **Control**: Once a decision is made, put controls in place to follow up and be sure the alternative you selected is actually working.

Group Decision-Making

Some decisions are yours to make on your own. But others need to be made in a group, especially if other people are affected by the result. When you have a problem with a person, it is especially important that you determine the outcome you want to achieve. Are you looking for revenge or are you looking for resolution? Are you looking for a compromise or are you looking for a solution? What are you willing to give up to get what you want? For example, if you are living in a multiple-person environment, your roommates may also need to be part of the decision making.

Decision-making is a process that is determined by the challenge itself. If the decision to be made will affect others, you need to bring them into the process of making the decision. One of the best ways to secure cooperation is to solicit input from those involved. The advantages of having the group take a part in the process is that you will have greater cooperation in implementing the decision made if everyone participates in the choice. There will be less friction and greater commitment from everyone. The disadvantage is that it will take more time.

One way to conduct group decision-making is through brainstorming. This is done by allowing each person in the group to throw out any idea that comes to mind, and the moderator writes the ideas on a list for all to see. No criticism is allowed at this stage in the process and no ideas are considered "bad.". The ideas are not evaluated; they are merely presented. After all the ideas are on the table, each idea can be grouped in like sections and discussed by the group. Many will be eliminated quickly as they were just a quick thought. For the options remaining, make a list of the advantages and disadvantages of each alternative and filter them through a process similar to the attached **Decision-Making Alternative Diagram.**

Once you have selected an alternative, take the time to determine the best strategy to implement the decision. The implementation must include exact details of each task (knowing who has the authority to do the job) and a follow-up system to monitor the progress. Some of the challenges with group decisions are that more time is required of the leader to select a group and you must put in place the formal system needed for follow-up. The group must be closely directed as conflict can sometimes arise when all do not agree with the choices made. (Be aware, this method takes longer to actually make the decision than if you did it yourself. However, the cooperation you receive by having others input their advice is likely to make the whole process run more smoothly and require less time in the long run.)

Individual Decision Making

You will be the one to make the final decision if you are the only one affected by the decision or if you are the person selected to do so. The process of making a decision on your own is exactly the same as for the group:

- You must provide the time,
- Evaluate the situation,
- Come up with alternatives,
- Filter the alternatives through the decision-making process, and
- Come up with a solution to implement and monitor.

The obvious advantage of you making the decision is that you don't have to wait for other's input, and you have total control of the decision made. If you are the only one to make the decision, right or wrong, you must live with the results of the decision you make. (A mentoring team could be very effective and valuable here.) When this is the case there are several rules to follow:

- Learn from past decisions made.
- Be willing to try something new.
- Actively seek help from outside mentors.
- Be aware of your own priorities and values. Will this decision support your ethics?
- Be aware of how other people will be affected by the decision. Will it be fair to them?
- Will you sleep well tonight after making this decision?

Attached you will find **a Decision-Making Test** that may help with your selection. If you are comfortable with your answers to each of the questions, you should be happy with the decision itself.

It doesn't matter which side of the fence you get off on sometimes.
What matters most is getting off.
You cannot make progress without making decisions.
Jim Rohn

Decision-Making Alternatives

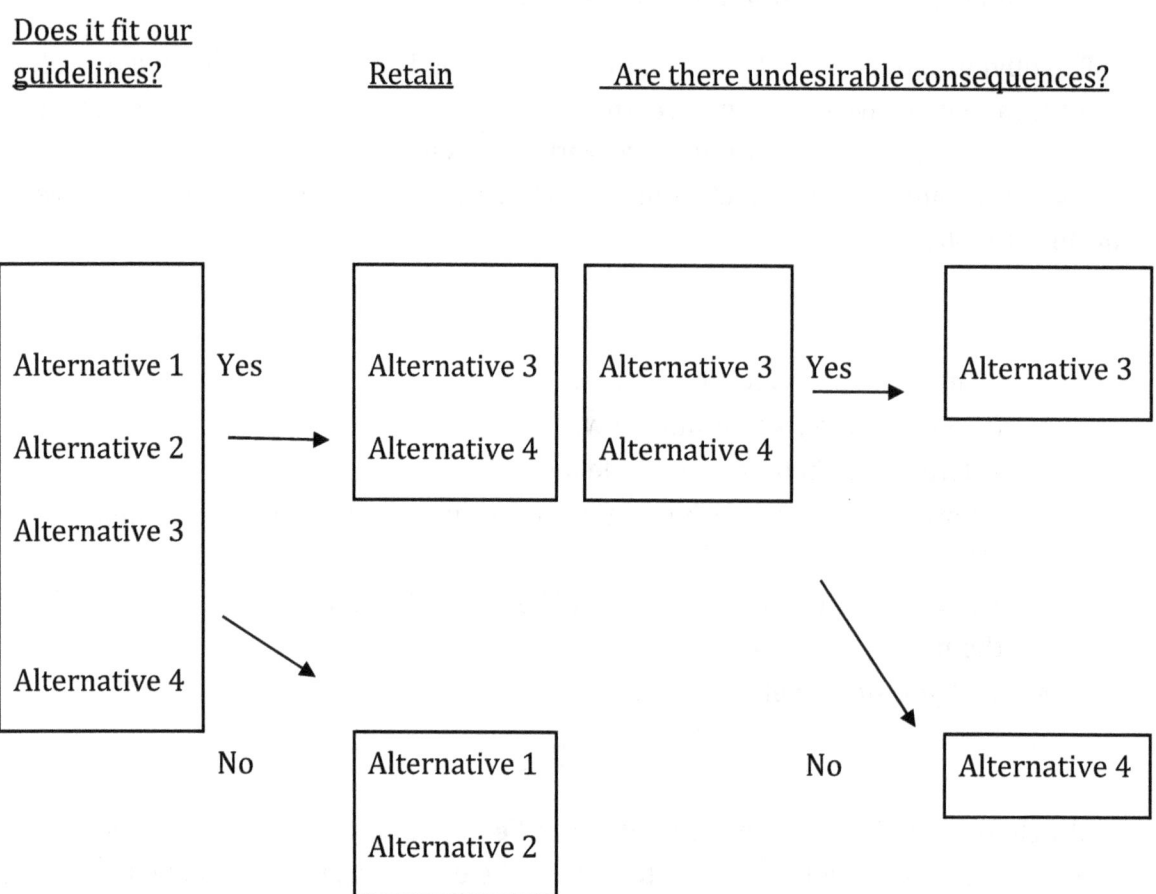

Decision-Making Test

There are several questions to ask yourself about the decision you select:

1. Would I be embarrassed for my family to know this decision?

    Yes ☐   No ☐

2. Would I be happy if someone else made this decision for me?

    Yes ☐   No ☐

3. Does this decision adversely infringe on anyone else?

    Yes ☐   No ☐   If so, who? _____

4. Does this decision benefit on an unbiased basis?

    Yes ☐   No ☐

5. Would I make this decision even if I did not benefit from it?

    Yes ☐   No ☐

6. Will this decision cause harm to someone else?

    Yes ☐   No ☐   If so, who? _____

7. Will I sleep well tonight knowing I have made this decision?

    Yes ☐   No ☐

Next you will find a ***Decision-Making Skills Assessment*** sheet that should help you become aware of the things you need to know (or learn) with reference to making decisions. If you implement each of these points, you will improve your decision-making abilities. Notice that decision making is a learned skill – which means that you can become good at it if you put forth the effort to learn. The goal of this model is not to determine your score; but to help you determine which areas of your decision-making abilities need work.

Decision-Making Skills Assessment

This questionnaire will evaluate your current decision-making skills. If you do not have experience in a management position, then evaluate yourself with regard to a group you have worked with either in the classroom or in an organizations, church, or service group.

Use the following scale to rate the frequency with which you perform the behaviors described in each statement. Place the appropriate number (1-7) in the blank space:

Rarely	Irregularly	Occasionally	Usually	Frequently	Mostly	Always
1	2	3	4	5	6	7

____ 1. I identify opportunities or diagnose problems by collecting data.

____ 2. I identify the objectives and put a measurable plan in place to diagnose them.

____ 3. I generate many alternatives for solving the problem.

____ 4. I solicit advice from those who will be involved in the solution.

____ 5. I look for methods that have been used before to solve similar problems.

____ 6. I list both positive and negative aspects of alternative decisions.

____ 7. I consider how each alternative will affect others.

____ 8. I select an alternative based on data, input of others, and past experience.

____ 9. I support my choices with facts.

____ 10. I provide resources and establish time frames as part of my strategy.

Emotional Intelligence
Controlling feelings is a choice.
What you feel is not nearly as important
as what you do with how you feel.

Emotional Intelligence is simply using the emotions you have to help you discern the situation you are in and turn the situation into an opportunity to grow; as well as reading the emotions of others so you can help them grow.

Positive vs. Negative Emotions

Positive	**Negative**
Trusting	Scared/Worried
Happy	Hurt
Confident	Embarrassed
Glad	Sad
Excited	Anxious
Ecstatic	Depressed
Pleased	Sorry
Confident	Reserved
Proud	Guilty
Amazed	Defeated
Determined	Resistant
Free	Controlled
Love	Apathetic

From personality studies we know that negative emotions come from fear, hurt and embarrassment; and most people do not want to admit those feelings, so they blame, get angry, withdraw, or procrastinate to regain control of the situation – none of which works.

When you understand that you have the ability to control your emotions – rather than your emotions controlling you – you put yourself in a position of power. Losing control means you lose. Understanding emotions helps you navigate society. You are no longer reacting to the person, but to the feeling in the person.

Four Basic Abilities of Emotional Intelligence:

1. **The ability to recognize and identify emotions in oneself and in others.** This is done from facial expressions, voice recognition, pictures, and even knowledge of cultures. (Without this ability, one cannot go further with emotional growth.)
2. **The ability to use emotions to one's best advantage to solve problems and think through processes.** Example: Fear causes a fight-or-flight response. Emotional Intelligence helps determine which action is best.
3. **The ability to understand emotions to help you sense what you are feeling before it gets out of control and to hear a change of emotion as it occurs.**
4. **The ability to manage emotions in order to maintain control.** You cannot manage someone else's emotions, but you can manage your reaction to them, and that often changes their emotions and yours.

Managing your emotions when you are young has been proven to improve your performance when you mature. When testing four-year-olds to see how they react with reference to instant gratification, studies show that those children who were able to wait for a reward in their youth, in their teen years scored on average 210 points higher on the college Standard Achievement Test (SAT) tests.

What you need to succeed in controlling emotions:

1. **Self-awareness.** Know your own strengths and weaknesses. Set your own goals and identify your values. Recognize how your desires affect others you deal with.
2. **Self-regulation.** Adapt to change, control your reactions and redirect your negative emotions.
3. **Social Skills.** Manage your relationships to help move them in a positive direction.
4. **Empathy.** See the world through another's eyes. Especially when making decisions for yourself.
5. **Motivation.** Drive yourself to succeed and control yourself.

Emotional Intelligence is hard to measure, which means it is not a pure science. It is more a skill, talent, or tool – not to be used as a manipulation of others. Different personalities will be instinctively better or worse than others in some areas of Emotional Intelligence.

- The personality most likely to understand and control emotions will be the laid-back Phlegmatic.
- The one least likely to show and respond to emotions outwardly is the most-introverted Melancholy.
- The one with the most difficulty controlling negative responses is the high-powered Choleric.
- The one most likely to express the most emotions will be the fun-loving Sanguine.

It is not just important to know how to react emotionally, but to actually follow through with appropriate behavior, which takes control. Bullying and victimization are signs of poor Emotional Intelligence. Counseling and caring are traits of higher Emotional Intelligence.

A 2010 study showed that Emotional Intelligence improved significantly with the reduction of substance abuse and self-esteem increased in the same proportion.

10 Ways to Improve Your Emotional Intelligence:

1. Spend some time every day evaluating and identifying your emotions. When you feel uncomfortable in a conversation, resist the desire to change the subject or interrupt. Follow through to reach understanding.
2. Don't judge your emotions before you evaluate them. Emotions are often healthy warning signs. They can keep you out of trouble and pain.
3. When emotions rise, see if you can connect them to past events that may or may not still be relevant. Leave the past in the past.
4. Connect your feelings with your thoughts. Is the emotion you are feeling a result of what is happening, what happened in the past, or what you imagine is going to happen?
5. Listen to your body. A knot in your stomach may be a sign of stress. Butterflies are often a sign of excitement, pleasure, or fear.
6. Ask others how you are coming across in your relationships. Be sure it is someone you can trust to be honest and who knows you well.
7. Become more aware of your unconscious feelings.
8. Ask yourself how you feel. Your feelings should not be in control, but should be considered as warning signs.

9. Keep a journal of your feelings until you learn how to identify them through your body language and how to control them with your thoughts.
10. Learn when to shift your thoughts from yourself to others. Don't dwell on the negative. Once you have identified and controlled your emotions, move toward using that knowledge to help someone else.

Culture and Emotions:

Culture and emotions are related. All cultures know that violence is wrong, but some cultures have a higher tendency to control the emotions that lead to violence than others. For example, countries where citizens must protect themselves, as opposed to having a government in place that helps, have a higher tendency to react more quickly and have less guilt associated with the action.

Even culture in our country is different from north and south of the Mason-Dixon Line:

- Studies show that 36% of Southerners approve of killing to protect their family versus 18% of Northerners.
- Northerners are more likely to be violent over property (home, car, etc.) and Southerners over people (divorce, etc.).

People from a herding society are more likely to be violent than city dwellers – probably because they have to defend their cattle, sheep, etc.

Emotions came from personalities, environment, families, societies (cultures), past experience, and levels of education and intelligence. You cannot control another's emotions, but you can influence them through your own reactions.

Emotional control is a lifetime project. It is improved by knowledge, effort, and persistence. Hopefully, control of our emotions increases with age and experience. Life is more enjoyable and less stressful when emotions are used successfully.

Emotional Intelligence

Identify the basic emotions that disturb you the most (frustration, fear, anger, etc.).

_____

_____

_____

What are the main triggers for these emotions? (Injustice, discrimination, betrayal, etc.)

_____

_____

_____

What actions can you put in place to help you become a better listener so you can understand another's emotions?

_____

_____

_____

Think of a conflict in your past that you feel you did not handle well. What changes would you make should you be faced with the same issue again?

_____

_____

_____

_____

_____

_____

Forgiveness

*"Forgiveness is a beautiful word
until we have someone to forgive."*
(C. S. Lewis)

All of us, at different times in our lives, need to either forgive or ask for forgiveness. It is part of the human heart to transgress. We know our need for divine forgiveness is infinitely greater than any forgiveness we might ever be called on to extend to others. Any sin against another always involves a greater sin against God. No wonder David said: *"Blessed is he whose transgression is forgiven, whose sin is covered"* (Psalm 32:1 KJV). When we understand that the same evil that motivated our offender to hurt us also resides in our own heart, we are in a much better position to forgive.

Philip Carlson said, *"We bring with us into every new day the memories and experiences of the past."* Forgiving and forgetting are two different things. We don't necessarily need to or even have the ability to forget, for remembering is a learning experience, but we must learn to forgive. And the main person we must forgive is ourselves. I believe it was James Long who said, *"One reason God created time was so that there would be a place to bury the failures of the past."*

To forgive does not mean to forget. We learn from our life experiences. Denial of the past simply assures repetition in the future. **Forgiveness does not deny the seriousness of the event.** Christ did not become evil to bare our guilt, and we do not have to become perfect to receive His forgiveness. Forgiveness requires that we set aside our own feelings, accept the wrong of another, and not demand our due. It is the offended who is to turn the other cheek, offer his coat as well as his shirt, and walk the extra mile.

Forgiveness does not mean there will be no consequences for the injury. It simply means that you will not allow the hurt to continue to hurt you into the future. An offense always creates an obligation, and someone has to pay:

- When we forgive another, we acknowledge there is a wrong
- We recognize there is a price to pay
- And we choose to cover the loss ourselves

Many hold on to forgiveness because they are unaware that the debt they hold is really worthless – very few offenders have the resources to pay for their offense.

To not forgive is like taking poison and expecting the other person to die. Unforgiveness hurts you. In many cases, the person you need to forgive either is unaware of any transgression or simply does not care. Therefore, your forgiveness does not affect them. Sometimes the person you need to forgive is no longer living. In this case, it is obvious that the benefit of forgiveness does not go to the offender.

There is a difference between granting forgiveness and receiving forgiveness. You can grant forgiveness whether it is received or not. Look at the offender as a rattlesnake. When you pick up a rattlesnake you expect it to bite. That is what a rattlesnake does. To let go of a rattlesnake benefits the snake, but it benefits you as well.

God's word tells us we must free ourselves from anything that distracts us from serving Him. Forgiveness is the obligation of the forgiven. Those who refuse to forgive enter their own private torture chamber. While the pain someone has inflicted on us is real, it is nothing compared to the wrongs we have committed against God. We forgive to be forgiven. And, if God **commands** us to do it, He will **help** us through it.

Forgiveness means, once we have done all we can do, once God has forgiven us and we have sincerely asked for forgiveness, we can go forward without guilt. No longer should we allow that incident to control our emotions. Each time it crosses our mind, we need to say, *"Thank You for forgiving me and allowing me to forgive,"* and move forward, knowing we are forgiven. Forgiveness is either to start over or to let go. If you cannot say "I forgive you", say "I am letting you go" or "let's start over".

There can be forgiveness without reconciliation. But there is no reconciliation without forgiveness. A healthy relationship cannot survive in an unforgiving state. The world and our media tell us that revenge is ours, God says it is His (Romans 12:17-19).

If the decision is to start over, then the forgiveness includes letting go of the past transgression. However, not all forgiveness needs to, or even should, include reconciliation. Some forgiveness simply means we let go of the relationship, without carrying the bitterness of unforgiveness into the future. If there is anyone you need to forgive **OR** any reason you need to be forgiven, **NOW** is the best time to address the issue before it has time to fester in your heart – or in theirs.

The people we are most likely to offend or be offended by are those we care the most about. We are far more likely to get upset with a parent, spouse, or child, than we are with the neighbor down the street. The greater the love connection, the more emotional the offense will be, and the more difficult to let it go. Hurt makes it difficult to rebuild a relationship, but unforgiveness makes it impossible. Love means always being willing to say, "I'm sorry."

One reason forgiveness is so difficult is that we have a tendency to feel our transgressions are not as bad as another's. We judge others more strictly than we judge ourselves. We justify our actions as excusable and blame others for theirs. Forgiveness is hard if we try to do it on our own, but it is easy if we turn to our Higher Power.

It is also important to recognize that whether the other party accepts our forgiveness or not is irrelevant. God does. He has promised that: *"If my people, which are called by My name, shall humble themselves, and pray, and seek my face, and turn from their wicked ways; then will I hear from Heaven, and will forgive their sin, and will heal their land"* (2 Chronicles 7:14 KJV).

Forgiveness must be real. Although our good works might be useful in hiding the true condition of our souls to others, they are absolutely useless in the sight of God. *"When we genuinely forgive, we set a prisoner free, and then discover that the prisoner we set free was us"* (Lewis Smedes).

REPENTANCE:

Repentance is vitally important to accepting forgiveness, but irrelevant to giving forgiveness. Repentance is a change of mind that leads to a change of direction. Genuine repentance will show up in behavior. Repentance involves acknowledging you are wrong. True guilt is an indicator that something is wrong in our life. (But beware: there are two kinds of guilt in this world. One that pushes us to change our behavior; and one that is put on us just to make us suffer and feel bad – so don't fall into the trap of feeling guilty if you have not done anything wrong.) Repentance is the offender's responsibility; forgiveness is the responsibility of the offended.

Repentance is not something we can demand. It must be freely given. If we demand repentance, remorse, or rehabilitation from us or from the offender, we are emotionally stagnated.

CONSEQUENCES:

When we seek vengeance, we have a desire to see another person suffer for the pain he/she has caused us. Justice, on the other hand, is the payment God or others might demand from someone because of a wrong they have committed. Justice is allowing someone else to settle the score.

One of the greatest barriers to forgiveness is the myth that forgiveness automatically frees our offender from any consequences for actions. Consequences are necessary because they promote order in society and deter others from the same poor behavior. Negative consequences can be a deterrent to evil. God uses consequences to bring us back into a right relationship with Him and to help keep us there. Once an offense is made, a consequence must be paid.

FORGETTING:

Even though forgiveness happens, repentance takes place, and consequences are paid, the scars remain. A nail driven in a board can be removed, but the hole still remains as a reminder – that is why we don't forget. Forgetting is impossible and not profitable. Remembering keeps us from repeating the same transgression – or from allowing the same transgression against us. One reason God allows us to remember our sin is so we might consider and recall His undeserved grace. Recalling our own mistakes keeps us humble. Allowing God to handle mistakes against us is also a sign of humility and maturity.

Healing can come with the passing of time, but usually only after proper surgery and treatment. Unfortunately, there is no rewind button in life. To grant forgiveness, we must first receive forgiveness from God and others.

Wounds of the past can never be changed, but they can be healed, and forgiveness is God's tool to accomplish the healing.

Forgiveness Questions

The number one person you must forgive is yourself, and most of us have many things to forgive. What do you need to forgive most about yourself?

_____

_____

_____

Make a list of anyone you need to forgive. Write down what you will specifically forgive them for.

_____

_____

_____

_____

Then make a list of all those things you want to be forgive for. (In any case where you can, ask forgiveness of the person you offended and make whatever amends you can.)

_____

_____

_____

_____

Take both lists out in the field, set them on fire and, watch your pain go up in smoke.

Goal Setting
Finding your Purpose and
Taking your Dreams from Vision to Reality
Man is here for the sake of other men.
Albert Einstein

You have the tools you need to succeed. You have a good mind and a great heart. You can create the life you want if you put in place goals to get you there. You simply have to decide to continue as you are – especially if you are happy with your life– or to make a change if you are not happy. Do what you need to do. Identify your purpose and your talents and put a plan in place. Do the research necessary and have faith in yourself and your Creator.

Purpose

Everything created has a purpose – including you and me. Originally, everything was created from nothing. But from that point on, everything was created from a seed, and in that seed was everything needed to make that plant or animal exactly what it should be. Denis Kimbro, in his book **Think and Grow Rich: The Black Choice**, said: *"The fundamental law of the universe is that every form of life holds within itself every element it needs for growth, maturity, and development."* Everything is found in the seed and the seed is created for a reason.

Only to the extent that we serve others will we know our purpose for living. And only when we identify our purpose can we fulfill it. You need to know your purpose, know what makes you happy, and what you do well. What do you love to do? What would you volunteer to do if you could? What comes easily for you? What things are others often asking you to help them with? What makes you excited to get up in the morning? Answering these questions helps you identify your talents and identify how you can use your talents to help others.

Identify your talents

One way to identify your talents is to determine what things you do that are so easy you discount their value. Things that are easy for you may be very hard for another, for all of us are different. An over-active personality is often in need of an organizer, and the organizer is in need of a project.

Malcolm X says, *"We should give life our best – let us use our lives more wisely to chase our dreams, find our true purpose, and be as happy and successful as possible."* If you know what you want, if you are determined to get it (to the point that it becomes an obsession), and you back that obsession with continuous effort and sound planning, then you have discovered your true purpose.

But knowing what you should be doing - knowing what is important to you - is of no value without action. Direction is not of any use to the person who is not moving. God expects us to do what we can. He will then do what we cannot. If we are not doing our part, God is limited as to what He will do. He is our guide not our chauffeur. I have a plaque on my office wall that says, **"Don't ask God to guide your footsteps, if you are not willing to move your feet."**

If you know your purpose and are working to fulfill it, nothing can stop you from reaching your goals. The goal itself will create passion. The key to passion is having a purpose. With passion and purpose, success is inevitable.

Don't be surprised if you find yourself holding back on discovering your purpose. It is not an easy task. It takes time, faith, and courage to find it and to fulfill it. Courage is simply faith put in action. Courage opens the door to a warehouse of power, and faith only works in the present. We will not be given a purpose that our Creator is unwilling to fulfill.

Define your future

To find your purpose you have to visualize your future. Once you see it, you can believe it, and you can create it. Goals simply bring the future into the present. Spend time every day reviewing what you want to accomplish in life and what steps you need to take to get the job done. Dreams are illusive until you make them real and the best way to make them real is to write them down.

Make a list of the accomplishments you want to make in life. Then identify them by priority. "A" priority items are those tasks that are truly important to you. "B" projects are those things you would like to get done. And "C" items are those things you would like to do if time is left over and resources are available. Once the list is made, take all the "A" priorities and list them on a separate sheet. Then do the same prioritization in 1, 2, 3 order. The items that you rate as "A-1" will help you identify your real purpose. Those are the things that must be done for you to feel successful and use your God-given talents.

You will never rise above your ability to see your future. We are always moving ahead in life or falling behind. There is no standing still. We are not promised any day but today. If we want to fulfill our purpose, today is the only time to start.

From Vision to Reality

Goals are what wake you up in the morning and keep you going all day long. But, if you don't know where you want to go, you will go in the direction the world pushed you. Building a life takes discipline, persistence, determination, self-motivation, WORK and CHANGE! To make a change you need a reason. Your goals are the driving force to take you to success. Once you can identify what you want from life, you can work toward accomplishing it. But to have the motivation to work, you have to know your WHY. What will you get from accomplishing these goals?

To help you set your goals, you need to know your talents. What talents do you have and what do you know that would be helpful to others?

- What are you good at?
- What do you like to do?
- What do others ask you to do?
- What did you want to grow up to be?

Success will come when you are working in an area you are talented in. *"You have not learned to live, until you have found what you are willing to die for"* (Martin Luther King, Jr.). So, what do you want to be remembered for?

One of the best ways to determine what character traits are important to you is to identify what you like best in someone else, then work to create the same character in you. You have to be able to see where you want to go before you can believe you can get there. Zig Ziglar says, *"You cannot consistently perform in a manner that is inconsistent with the way you see yourself."*

To use your talents and fulfill your mission, you have to have goals: personal, family/friend, and career goals. Here are some examples and resources you can use to learn how to set goals: Zig Ziglar's **Top Performance** and Benjamin Franklin's **Autobiography of Benjamin Franklin.**

You need <u>personal goals</u> in the areas of spiritual, character, health, education, and finance. Your <u>family/friend goals</u> need to incorporate how you enhance, build, and maintain relationships. Some things to consider are:

- Set a goal to call a friend once-a-month
- Set a goal to write a letter once-a-quarter to a friend at a distance
- Read a book to the children in your life before they go to sleep each night
- Create a game-night with family and/or friends
- And always count the costs

<u>Career goals</u> include the position you want to hold and the money you want to create.

Expand your vision. *"He that is good at making excuses is seldom good at anything else"* (Benjamin Franklin). Once you know what you want for your life, break it down into little pieces. In his book **Top Performance**, Zig Zigler gives you seven steps to setting goals. They are:

1. Identify the goal
2. List the benefits to accomplishing it
3. Identify the obstacles in the way
4. Identify the skills and knowledge you need to acquire
5. Identify who can help
6. Put together a step-by-step plan
7. Set a time to complete the goal

After completing the goal, follow up to be sure you have accomplished what you wanted to accomplish. *"The only activity that will ever help you succeed is the one you do"* (Skip Ross).

Try an experiment: Close your eyes and imagine that all your bills are paid, and you are bringing in an additional $1,000 a month over and above what you are currently receiving. (You can change the amount to $5,000 or any other number that works for you.) Then ask yourself the following questions:

Where would you live? _____

Where would your parents or guardians live? _____

What kind of car would you drive? _____

Where would your children (grandchildren) go to school? _____

Would you continue your education? _____ Where? _____

What would you study? _____

Where would you go on vacation? _____

What charity or church would you support? _____

How would you support them? Mission? Money? _____

Who else would you help? _____ How? _____

What kind of work would you do? _____

"Once you have a plan in place, all you have to do is follow it."

Here are some insightful quotes from a book called <u>**What Keeps Me Standing**</u> by Dennis Kimbro. Thought you might enjoy them:

"From the day you are born until your eyes close in death, learn something new every day."
Katie Adams 80+

"It is better to look forward and prepare than to look back and regret."
Laura Moss 80+

"There is something in you that is greater than what is holding you back."
Lucille Singleton 80+

"Hope is believing in abundance while staring poverty in the face."
Frances Diaz 80+

Here's to you. Keep Smiling!

Purpose Questions

What are the things you know you do well?

_____

_____

_____

What is one thing you do that makes you excited to get up in the morning?

_____

_____

List the top three most important tasks you would like to accomplish in order:

_____

_____

_____

If you only had one year to live, what would you spend it doing?

_____

_____

_____

_____

_____

_____

_____

Identify a Goal

Identify one or more goals in each of these areas of your life and then work through the 7-step plan identified by Zig Ziglar.

Spiritual

_____

_____

Character

_____

_____

Health

_____

_____

Education

_____

_____

Finance

_____

_____

Other

_____

_____

_____

_____

Job Readiness
Preparation is the key to performing well!

Steps to take when you are ready to enter the job force:

Before:
- Identify your strengths and weaknesses and your goals and values.
- Know what you like to do and what you do not like to do.
- Make sure you have the clothes you need to perform the job.
- Create a resume that highlights the experience you have that accommodates this job (You may create a different resume for each different position you apply for). If past experience is not important to this job, you do not have to list it. Take two copies of your resume with you.
- Create a cover letter with your resume that explains you and your situation. If you are seeking to change careers, explain in the cover letter any new training you have and how you use your past experiences to show what you have learned for your new direction.
- Contact former employers, friends, or associates to request references in writing and alert them that they may get a call.
- Research the businesses in your area to see who needs the talents you have and send your resume – whether they are advertising for anyone or not.
- Work out your transportation options before you set an interview. You have to be able to get to the job.
- Prepare questions before the interview that you would like to ask but save salary questions for after the job is offered. Example:
    - ✓ Do you have on-the-job training? Or do you provide for education?
    - ✓ What would a typical workday look like? And who would I be working with?

- ✓ Is there room for advancement in this position?
- Get a good night's rest.

Preparation is the key to performing well in an interview!

Morning of the Interview:

- Be neat, clean, confident, cheerful, and excited for an opportunity.
- Know you only want this job if it is the best fit for you and for the company. So, "no" simply means it was not the best fit.
- No thoughts of failure only of progress. This job is either meant for you or another is. Just work your way to the one that is best for you.

The Interview:

An interview is simply a discussion with a potential company to determine if you are the best person for the job and if the job is the best one for you. When you go for the interview:

- Dress appropriately according to the research you have done; business casual is usually the best option for anything other than a top management position.
- Be on time or early. Know beforehand where you are going. Get clear directions.
- Be totally honest – no matter what result it may cause.
- Use NO slang language in the interview or on the job.
- Sit up straight, take deep breaths, and control your nerves. This is not a life-or-death situation. You are sitting in a chair in an office – not in a fox hole.
- Don't rush your answers. If you need to think about it, DO!
- Stick to the interview. Do not bring up personal or controversial topics. This is business.
- Don't discuss salary before you are offered the job. If the interviewer asks you what salary you are looking for, use the research you have done and give them a high end of what you know you can perform and the industry is paying and say you are willing to start lower and be reviewed in 90 days to see that you qualify for the higher salary.
- Do not criticize a former employer or colleague. Do not BLAME or JUSTIFY your past. It is what it is! Just explain your progress if it comes up.

After the interview:

- Send a thank you note. Send it even if all you can say is "Thank you for your time."

Go prepared with a blank card and stamped, return-addressed envelope. Get a business card from your interviewer and write the note, address the card, and mail it as soon as you leave the interview.
- Three days later send a follow-up email asking if they need any additional information from you and requesting where they stand with making a decision.

Hard Questions:

- If you were fired or laid off from a job: Explain briefly why and what you learned from the experience without criticizing anyone involved in the dismissal.
- If you have not worked for a while: Show the progress you have made in your time off; your education, your career change, or illness.
- If asked how to handle a situation you have not experienced, state how you would handle it if it did happen and where you would get your answer and who you would go to for advice.
- If you are headed into a new career: Explain why you are making the change, what education you have received for the change, and why you want to make the change.

Miscellaneous:

- Research the company you will be interviewing and know what the company is looking for. Think of ways your talents could take them to the next level. What makes you feel you are the best person for this job?
- Where do you see yourself in five years? Will this company take you there?
- Accept your abilities and be proud of them. Stand up for yourself.

Don't panic. This is just a job!

You only want the RIGHT opportunity to open for you.

Job Readiness

What are your work goals?

_____

_____

Where do you want to be in five years?

_____

_____

What area do you need to work in to assure you have good transportation?

_____

_____

What type of work do you want to do?

_____

_____

What are the biggest challenges you have faced in the workplace in the past: The people? The job? Feeling the job is valuable? The location? Trouble concentrating? Teamwork?

_____

_____

_____

What can you do to improve or prevent this in the future?

_____

_____

_____

Love Barriers
The Wisdom of Relationships
(Inspired by Dr. Larry Crabb's "*66 Love Letters*")

We can only develop relationships in freedom. It is not something that can be forced. It requires a clear head and an open heart. It requires a desire to share ourselves with others. Sometimes we are tempted to develop a relationship because we have a great need to be needed. We are looking for what we will get out of the relationship, rather than what we can put into it. Since we are all addicted to something, we are always looking for a way to satisfy our needs. There is a void within us that we need to fill, because we were created for relationships.

We will fight a win-lose battle with all kinds of temptations all of our lives; whether they are temptations of physical, mental, or spiritual needs or temptations of drugs and alcohol or food or work or sex or gambling or bad thoughts. What are we supposed to do when a favorite desire hits us with a serious need for relief, when we lose all sense of freedom to do what is right?

Temptation is like "*...floating along in a fresh-water stream doing nothing consciously wrong and, without warning, finding ourselves on a fast-moving river of delicious temptations, heading straight for the falls of misery with no desire to reverse course; and thinking of our Higher Power only brings on guilty anger.*" (Dr. Larry Crabb)

It feels like a compulsive force inside of us takes over the mind with lies, the heart with self-serving affections, and the will with unrelenting strength for us to control. We become more concerned with what is happening to us than what is happening in us. We can't see the corruption beneath the compulsion. It is a struggle to relieve a sense of incompleteness, a void that demands fulfillment.

Here is the problem: when we fail and the next temptation comes along, we don't any longer see the activity as wrong. The more often we commit the wrong, the less wrong it feels. We give in easier every time to the point that we have no desire to fight. We are seeking relief that our Higher Power does not appear to be willing to give, and we think He is the one wrong.

When any temptation strikes, we want relief NOW. We lose our ability to look past the temptation to the future blessing of overcoming. All we can see is the moment we are in. That preoccupation for instant gratification is the corruption we are dealing with. Our expectation of feeling what we want to feel now in this fallen world makes us want to feel what we will feel forever in Heaven – but we don't want to wait. We become impatient and selfish. (A lot like Abraham and Sarah.)

The desire for relief becomes more compelling than the desire to do the right thing – to be loving. We feel our void must be filled before we are able to love. When we live with a desire for instant cure, we become obsessed with loneliness that is not relieved quickly. If it were, we would not learn from it. The void within is a temptation to relieve the pain, heal the wounds, and restore peace. We are now living by the flesh and lose the freedom to love ourselves or others.

Developing relationships requires changing our focus from the past to the present. It requires letting go of the fear of pain that all relationships will bring. Faith in our Higher Power and hope for tomorrow frees us to love today. And love releases a joy within that nothing else can bring.

Relationships require commitment, loyalty, and presence. They require caring and loving and helping. They require compromise and forgiveness. To feel joy in our lives, it is imperative that we love others. We have the perfect example of a God Who loves us without reservation. He does not free us to follow temptations, but He does want us to know that we cannot out-sin His forgiveness. The rule in relationships is to focus more on loving than on resisting temptation.

"I am not free to do everything right – I can't. And I am not free to do whatever makes me feel complete – that's wrong. But I am free to love – and that freedom brings joy. ... Let the corruption within you become an occasion for humility and self-abasement that will release your desire to move toward others ... Make every effort not to sin less but to love more." (Dr. Larry Crabb)

Love Barriers
You must do the thing you think you cannot do.
Eleanor Roosevelt

What is the biggest temptation you face?

_____

_____

_____

What is the biggest reward you will receive when you overcome it?

_____

_____

_____

What activity can you do when the temptation comes to help you overcome?

_____

_____

_____

Organization

**Many opportunities are missed
because proper preparation is not made to receive them.
Organization allows for that preparation.**

Every farmer knows if you want to eat in the winter, you have to plant in the spring; and to plant in the spring, you must prepare in the winter. For a farmer, organization is the key to survival. Organization is simply preparing in advance; or, as Christopher Robin in **Management by Winnie the Pooh** says, "Organization is what you do before you do something, so when you do it, it won't be all messed up." Organization may be boring and difficult, but don't ever call it unimportant or unrewarding. You will recognize the benefit the first time you go looking for your keys, and you find them on the hook you hung for them.

To be truly organized, you should have a plan for every day, a place for everything, and everything in its place. A clean orderly place is uplifting and makes life a lot easier. The best way to keep it that way is to put things back where you found them.

Organization is important for several reasons:

- It makes you more productive
- It helps eliminate stress
- It saves time, work, and money
- It frees your mind to think of other things
- It reduces frustration

Organization is motivated by a plan and a desire. If there is something you want to accomplish, you will most likely succeed if you know the steps you need to take and the order you need to take them in. Most things of importance don't happen by chance but by preparation.

The historical character that I think most shows the importance of organization was Nehemiah. This is his story:

Nehemiah was told by his brother that the walls of Jerusalem, his home, were in ruins. At the time, he was the trusted cupbearer to the king of Babylon – an important position. The cupbearer not only served the king's wine, he tasted it to be sure it was safe to drink. He was also well known by the king, for when this news hit him, the king - without Nehemiah saying anything - realized he was in distress.

Nehemiah had a great desire to rebuild the walls of Jerusalem. His first step was prayer and his second was a plan. We know he had a plan because when the king asked Nehemiah what he wanted from him, Nehemiah gave him a list. When he arrived in Jerusalem, he assigned every portion of the wall to the appropriate builders for that section. As a result, the entire wall of Jerusalem was completed in 52 days, despite serious opposition.

Personal Organization:

The **first step** toward personal organization in today's world is a planner – a place where you can break down every step of your ventures into reasonable goals to be accomplished one piece at a time. The **second step** is a 12-month expandable file, and the **third step** is a file box or cabinet.

Make your plans and transfer the steps to your planner (whether paper or on your phone) on the day you will actually do the job. Part of organization is having written goals for every part of your life with a list of tasks to accomplish them. This is the main use for your planner. The more things you can get off your mind and into a planner, the more productive you will be and the clearer your mind will be for more important things than the to-do list. Know what you need to accomplish each month and break things down into what has to be done today. Often it works best to plan from the finished product backwards to determine when each activity must be completed.

You should only have **ONE** calendar that records everything. If your calendar is not your phone, but a paper calendar, it should be small enough to carry with you at all times and large enough to give you the details you need. Write down everything you need to do and every place you need to be. For appointments, include addresses and contact numbers. Review the calendar before going to bed every evening to be ready for the next day, and schedule a planning session once-a-week for the following week. If you have a partner, review each other's plans together so you can support each other and not double-book your appointments.

For your expanding file, at the beginning of each year, record all the birthdays and anniversaries (special days) you want to remember on the calendar. Have a list of all the important dates and pick up cards for every birthday, anniversary, or thank-you note you may need and put them in the appropriate month of your expanding folder, along with any tickets for events or reminders for maintenance. Then create folders for any expenses you need to track through the year for taxes.

Set up a file cabinet (or box) to hold all documents you need to keep, so they are not cluttered on your desk. Give them simple labels so you can find them easily.

Space Organization:

Plan the space you will be working in, so you don't have to jump up every few minutes to retrieve something. Having a specific area to do your paperwork trains your mind to focus better. It is best to have a door on the space, if possible, to keep out unwanted interruptions and to close when the work is done.

When you set up your filing system, keep it simple. Any bills or materials related to the household can go in a file labeled **HOME**. Anything with reference to the car can literally be labeled **CAR** or **MY CAR** if you have more than one. You can do the same with **INSURANCE**. You can also create a file for each individual in the family under their **NAME**.

Pick up a box and call it your *treasure chest*. Designate it for those special things you want to keep forever. This is not for every picture the children create for you. That goes in their file. This is for the last note from your mother or the ticket stubs from your first date or 25th anniversary.

Have special containers for each person in the house for all their toiletries (toothbrush, toothpaste, deodorant, etc.) that you don't want anyone else using. Each box can be a different color or pattern. The box can then be kept in the individual bedrooms and transported back and forth to the bathroom when needed. This will keep your counter in the bathroom clean.

Task Management:

Do first things first. Stop procrastination. Determine the most important things you need to get done and do them first. That way you can enjoy the rest of the day without guilt. **Praetor's Rule** (also known as the 80/20 Rule) says 80% of results is produced by 20% of effort. Know what your best 20% work time is and schedule yourself not to be interrupted in that time. With good organization you can improve your 20%, but that is what you have to start with. *"**Hours can be saved by making good use of minutes**"* (John Maxwell).

Keep on hand a list of things you can do in a few minutes; like making a phone call or writing a letter, or reading an article, and have on hand the supplies you need to do the job. Then use your wait time to get these things off the to-do list. Do what you can do every day to make tomorrow easier. Just because you can't do everything does not mean you don't do anything. The more organized you are the more you will get done.

Working from Home:

Working from home gives you flexible work hours that you must control. *"If you are currently working from home or considering it for the future, be aware that the very factors that make it so appealing are the same ones that make it difficult."* (Pat Roessle Materka: ***Time In Time Out Time Enough***). Let friends and family know when you will be working and ask that they not interrupt except for emergencies.

Disorganization is an excuse for not getting things done. The sooner you do something, the more time you will have to enjoy the result of your work and the more time you will have to correct any mistakes you may have made. *"Hard work is the accumulation of easy things you did not do when you should have"* (John Maxwell).

Prioritization:

What is important to your life? What do you do first, what do you do second.... How do you determine the priority? Have you determined the God-given talents you possess, and do you know how to use those talents to help you prioritize your life? If we do not use the talents we have been given, we are being unfaithful and ungrateful to the Giver.

Once you are able to visualize your perfect life, you will be able to identify your purpose and your mission. Just remember: *"You cannot consistently perform in a manner that is inconsistent with the way you see yourself"* (Zig Ziglar). What Zig Ziglar is saying in this quote is that you have to be able to see where you want to be before you can believe that you will ever get there.

C. Thomas Anderson says: *"God wants His people to have great wealth, because He has called them to do things that require much money."* To help determine the direction you should take with your life, answer the same questions you were asked in the Goal Setting chapter:

1. What do you like to do? (List three things)
2. What do you do well? (List three things)
3. As a child, what did you want to be when you grew up?
4. What do you feel is your strongest talent?

5. What do other people say you are good at?

Once you have answered the above questions, evaluate the results to see what talents show up the most often. Be particularly aware of what other people say you do well. It is so easy for us to overlook or underestimate the value of the things we do well naturally.

Once you have created a picture in your mind of what you want your life to look like and you have identified the people you want to share that vision with, you can start to identify the steps you need to take to achieve good organization.

"If one advances confidently in the direction of his dreams, and endeavors to live the life which he has imagined, he will meet with success unexpected in common hours."
-- Henry David Thoreau, Author

If you fail to take the action steps, you cannot expect to reach your goal. Stay focused on the benefit you will receive when the goal is accomplished and **NOT** on what you have to endure or eliminate in order to reach the goal. *Focus on what you get, not on what you have to give up.*

Organization makes most things easier!

Organization Homework

What time of the day are you most productive?

_____

What area or areas in your life need the most organization?

_____

_____

What is one thing you could do today that would make tomorrow easier?

_____

_____

What is one reward you could give yourself that would make you want to be organized?

_____

_____

Who do you know that might help you get organized?

_____

_____

Personality Traits
Summary of *"Personality Plus for Couples"*
by Florence Littauer

In order to work and live with others, it is necessary to know and understand yourself and how your personality affects others. Even though there are bad traits in all of us, **there are no bad personalities** and each personality is a combination of all personalities, for we are all unique and ***fearfully and wonderfully made*** (Psalm 139:14).

We are told to *"train up a child in the way he should go"* (Proverbs 22:6), and we think that means train him to know right from wrong and to do the right thing. That is part of it; but it also means to train him to be what he was created to be. Was he created to be outgoing and fun, a leader of the pack, a deep thinker, or a peacemaker? How was he specifically designed? What personality was he born with?

Every personality has potential to be productive and a blessing to others. Each personality can be a combination to bring glory to God. The reason we study personalities is to help us recognize that just because someone acts differently does not mean they are wrong. As a matter of fact, what we are most often attracted to in another is the opposite traits from those we possess. Opposites still attract.

Opposite personalities are designed to refine and build each other. You can become a better person if your partner in life or work is your opposite. Statistically, it is known that, when we make friends, we often are attracted to someone who is similar to us, but when we select a life partner, we are more often attracted to an opposite. The challenge then becomes, over time, do we continue to appreciate the other's strengths, or do we look at their opposite traits as weaknesses or wrong? If you are a doer, do you look at the peacemaker as wasting time? If you are a thinker, do you look at the outgoing individual as flighty? Or do you recognize that the combination of those personalities improves life experiences for everyone.

In our study of personalities, we are going to discover our most natural reactions to life's events – both positive and negative. We are going to learn how our personality affects others and why we react as we do to other personalities. We will discuss the benefits of each personality trait as well as the weaknesses and what causes the weaknesses to show up. As we learn, consider the analogy of opposites as a helium balloon with a string. We know that a helium balloon needs a string to keep it grounded, and every string is more fun and has greater purpose with a balloon attached to it.

So, let's talk about the different personalities. I will use the titles they were given by Hippocrates (460 BC – 370 BC), the Father of Western Medicine. The titles he used were **Sanguine**, **Choleric**, **Melancholy**, and **Phlegmatic**.

Let's look at the GOOD SIDE:

Sanguine: The Sanguine personality is the most extraverted of all the personalities. They are the people lovers. They have a great desire to please and to be pleased. This personality is fun-loving, joyful, motivational, and just plain nice to be around. If you are going to have a party, be sure to have at least one to liven up the event. They are bright and are usually the center of attention. Sanguines energize their homes and their businesses. They are known as "the Talker", and their motto is "Are we having fun yet?"

Choleric: This personality is also extraverted, but less so. They deal well with people, but are more accomplishment oriented than people lovers. Rather than having a focus on "fun," they have a focus on "let's get things done." This is the personality you want to have around if you have a tough job to do. They are the leaders. Cholerics think things through and take action. They are known as "the Doers" and their motto, like Nike, is "Just do it!"

Melancholy: This word means thoughtful. The Melancholy personality is the most introverted personality. They really like their alone time. Melancholies are the most analytical, the most organized, and the most serious of all the personalities. The information you get from them will almost always be accurate. They pay close attention to detail. They prefer perfection in everything they do. The Melancholy is known as "the Thinker" and their motto is "If you are going to do it, do it right!"

Phlegmatic: The Phlegmatic personality is also introverted to some extent, even though they work well with people. They are smart, but have a tendency to keep that fact to themselves. They have a soothing affect on others and are great listeners. Phlegmatics take life with a grain of salt and seldom get upset over the little things. They are people pleasers with a dry sense of humor, slow to anger, and it takes a crisis to make them react. They are known as "the Peacemakers" and their mottos is, "Don't sweat the small stuff!"

When all is well, these are the reactions you can expect to see. However, there is another side to each personality, and that other side appears when anyone gets hurt, scared, or embarrassed.

Now for the BAD SIDE:

Sanguine: This personality has difficulty maintaining focus. They don't like exercise, excessive work, or great levels of responsibility. They don't like problems. They are the least organized of all the personalities. When things don't go well, they have a tendency to get defensive and **blame** others and **justify** their own behavior. They need to think before they react.

Choleric: This is the highly volatile personality. They lash out with **angry** words and sometimes with fists. They have a difficult time controlling the volume of their voices. They are poor listeners. They feel their way is always right and they should be in control. They are painful to be around when they don't get their way. They like and need control, so they must work to humble themselves and give others credit.

Melancholy: When things go bad for the Melancholy, they become a turtle and pull their heads into their shell. They mumble their words and avoid others. It is impossible to communicate with them. They **withdraw** sometimes for long periods of time. There is no way to solve a problem without their consent and cooperation. They need to be reminded to open up to others, for they often get lost in themselves

Phlegmatic: When the Phlegmatic's peace is disturbed, they become very stubborn and **procrastinate**. They become passive-aggressive. They don't complain too much, they just don't perform. Their thought is, "If I don't do anything, they can't blame it on me." Thus, you will think the job is getting done and the deadline will pass. They need to communicate more clearly

> *"To dwell above with the saints we love, O that will be glory.*
> *But to dwell below with the saints we know,*
> *well, that's a different story!"*
> (Anonymous)

COMPROMISE:

The best way to help your personality become an asset and keep it from becoming a weakness for someone else is to be aware of it. You can be the strength someone else needs. However, blame, anger, withdrawal, and procrastination are all major roadblocks to successful relationships. All are poor ways of handling a challenge. No problems get solved handled with these techniques. The negative aspects of our personalities are the ones we must learn to control. Just because it is our natural tendency to react in these ways does not mean it must happen. We have the ability to put in place new techniques and new better ways of behavior. Otherwise, we are going to hurt people. It is best that we compromise, communicate, integrate, and meet with other's needs.

A man who is strong in discernment can easily become judgmental. A man who is strong in accepting others can easily err by tolerating serious error.

COMPATIBILITY TEST:

Because of adverse circumstances in life – lack of love, sibling rivalry, and/or a desire to please loving or demanding parents – we unconsciously change our birth personality to fit our situation and wind up with opposite personalities within ourselves. This **causes major internal conflict** and is not easily changed until it is recognized and confronted.

The combinations of Sanguine/Choleric and Sanguine/Phlegmatic personalities are compatible. They can co-exist in the same body nicely. The Sanguine and the Melancholy, on the other hand, are total opposites. You can't be extremely extraverted, disorganized, and highly excitable at the same time you are withdrawn, meticulous, and have everything in order. This is something your mind won't tolerate without giving you trouble.

At the same time, the combinations of Choleric/Sanguine and Choleric/Melancholy personalities are compatible; but the Choleric and Phlegmatic personalities conflict – the one being a very action-oriented, high-energy producer and the other being laid-back and peaceful. Cholerics seek change and Phlegmatics avoid it. They have little in common.

Having said that, people do test as Sanguine/Melancholy and Choleric/Phlegmatic. For example: if you have spent a significant amount of time in close proximity with someone you care greatly about, and you have a real desire to please them, often you will work to be more like what they want you to be; and that causes conflict within yourself – especially as you get older. The same is true if you have lived in a dictatorial situation and have feared not following the direction you were led into, you may find yourself conflicted.

WHY LEARN?

It is important to recognize that we need all personalities to keep this world and our lives on track. Go back to the balloon analogy. If approached correctly, each personality can enhance the other – especially the opposite. The Sanguine can bring some more fun into the Melancholy life and the Melancholy can bring some organization into the Sanguine. The Choleric can motivate accomplishments for the Phlegmatic and the Phlegmatic can calm the Choleric.

Whatever your personality, use your assets to benefit others and use others to cover, improve, and educate you on your weaknesses. Know that what you have been given is what is best for you. Don't underestimate your value because you are not like someone else.

For a more in-depth study on personalities, read any of Florence Littauer's books and take the Personality Traits Test found in each book for yourself.

When we face personality differences, we need to be sensitive to how the other person thinks. We need to seek to work out our differences, if possible, in a spirit of love and kindness. We should not let the enemy cause us to attack those whom God has put into our lives and given different personalities than He has given us.

Personality Traits Overview

What are your basic traits?

    Extravert or Introvert   _____

    Talker or Thinker   _____

    Doer or Follower   _____

    Listener or Interrupter   _____

    Screamer or Crier   _____

    Justifier or Withdrawer   _____

What is your basic reaction when you are hurt, scared, or embarrassed?

_____

_____

What is one thing other people do that drives you crazy?

_____

_____

What is one trait you admire most in another?

_____

_____

Reread the above and see if you can determine where you fit on the personality chart. Remember, **there is no such thing as a bad personality**. All of us are a combination, and all of us are unique.

Relationships
"To get the full value of joy, you must have someone to share it with."
(Mark Twain)

"Every person you touch will pass along to those they touch the result of being touched by you" (Cindy Trimm). It is your heritage to the next generation. Therefore, it is important that you determine what you want to pass along. What kind of person do you want to be and reflect to others? To answer that question, your first relationship development has to be with yourself. You have to have a solid love for who you are before you have the ability to love anyone else. It cannot be an act. It must be real. You are unique. As T.D. Jakes says: *"You were born an original; don't live a life as a poor replica of someone else."*

Remember: What you are is God's gift to you. What you become is your gift back to Him. Be yourself. *"You cannot consistently perform in a manner that is inconsistent with the way you see yourself"* (Zig Ziglar). If you see yourself as a failure, it is difficult to act as if you are successful. But if you see yourself as successful before you are successful, you become successful.

The view we have of ourselves affects our attitude, our behavior, and our view of others. So, acknowledge what you like and don't like about yourself. Forgive yourself for any past transgressions. Get rid of any bitterness you may have toward anyone. Correct what makes you feel bad about yourself. Only after you have done this do you have a chance of developing good relationships with others.

How you see yourself is a reflection of how you have been treated, what you have been told, and, more importantly, what you believe. If you continue to see the world through childhood glasses, your future will be your present. You have to open yourself up for possible hurt. Reaching out to others, even when it is uncomfortable, is the first step toward building relationships. New relationships are necessary to undo old learning.

"People who need people are the luckiest people in the world." We are all a part of the same body and we cannot survive as a separate entity. We need people. We need to share in other peoples' feelings and emotions. Isolation is devastating. We deny our need for relationships because we don't want to want what we think we can't have. As a result, we replace our need for people with other things that are not good for us (like sex, work, gambling, alcohol, drugs, etc.), and we stay so busy there is no room for anyone else in our lives.

Building relationships is difficult, because we form our view of relationships before we have the mental capability to reason with our minds and we develop defenses from the family we are raised in. Making good human connections when you are raised without them takes a large dose of grace, trust, and time. Knowing how to recognize potential bad connections when you are raised in a sheltered environment is equally as hard.

Relationships take time and effort. Friendships can be risky and painful, but to find one that works is worth all the challenges you go through to establish it. Bob Marley said: *"The truth is everyone is going to hurt you. You've just got to find the ones worth suffering for."* It is important to identify for yourself the traits in a relationship that are important to you, so you will recognize them in others. For example:

- A person who is always late is not respecting your time. It could be that they don't appreciate their own time, or they have not been taught to respect others. But if time is important to you, you want timely relationships.
- A person who is bossy or talking down to you does not respect your mind. People don't change people. We can only change ourselves. Don't expect the respect to come just because you become friends.
- A person who is using profane language is not respecting your God. This may mean their beliefs are not the same as yours.
- A person who is asking for inappropriate affection is not respecting your body. This may be an indication their morals are not the same as yours.

It is equally as important that you also respect others' time, mind, God, and body. We should not ask for what we are not willing to give in a relationship. If these things are not important to you, they may not be an offense, but you do need to determine what is important to you and learn how to set good boundaries.

A person's character can be determined by their actions and reactions toward us. We all have a tendency to think that most people are like us. Therefore, if we are honest and kind, we expect the same from others. So, if you are dealing with someone who feels others are dishonest, it could be a sign that they have been mistreated enough that they have trust issues or it could also mean that they themselves are dishonest. If their behavior irritates us, Carl Jung said, *"Everything that irritates us about others can lead us to an understanding of ourselves."*

When developing relationships, take the best from others and give the best you have to give; but don't expect the exchange to be equal. Some people don't have the same ability to give as you have. Prior relationships affect and shape new ones. Past injuries, distorted thinking, and defense mechanisms are all a result of an imperfect world. Part of what prevents us from making connections is our concern about making a mistake and looking for perfection in others. Defenses are necessary and important when you are in an unsafe environment, but you have to release them in safety if you want to change. Change only takes place in safety. To grow yourself, you have to get out of your comfort zone. But to grow relationships, you have to create a comfort zone.

If you have had good relationships in the past, it is easier to build new one. If, on the other hand, you have often been hurt or betrayed, it is more difficult to allow yourself to bond with another. Be careful not to base your opinion of a new person on the treatments you have received in the past.

Types of Relationships:

Some relationships are casual and even temporary. Some are only for a season and others are for a lifetime. But all relationships are based on mutual respect and caring, and all relationships teach us something. Getting to know people opens our mind to what is most important to us. We learn what behaviors make us happy and which ones are irritating. The main relationships for most people are God, Spouse, Family, Friends, Co-workers/Roommates, Acquaintances, and Enemies. Let's discuss them individually in reverse:

- **Enemies:** *"Do not make friends with an angry man"* (Proverbs 22:24). However, you must love him. You don't have to spend time with him, but you must refrain from gossip. You must be kind; you must care and show caring. Martin Luther King, Jr. said: *"Love is the only force powerful enough to turn an enemy into a friend."*
- **Acquaintances:** These are usually people you may see seldom and don't know well. It is easy to misjudge someone you don't know – especially if they have a personality different from yours. This relationship usually starts off casual but may develop into more if enough time and effort is given. This could also be the relationship most affected by you - with very little knowledge on your part.

- **Co-Workers/Roommates:** These are people who are often chosen for you. You have to spend time with them, and you have to get along with them if you want a tranquil life. Making the time to understand what is important to them and trying to help cure their needs will take tension out of your daily life. Learning to express your own needs pleasantly is essential to partnership in this situation.
- **Friends:** These are the people you choose - people you can relax around and feel good being with. They make you happy and excited about life. They make life worthwhile. Everyone needs a friend. A friend is someone you respect, who also respects you, someone you can depend on in rough times. A friend is someone whose morals and values support yours, someone who listens, and someone with whom you have mutual affection. Most friends have similar personalities, share common interest, and, even though some friendships today are developed online or over distance, most friendships are at some point initially close enough in proximity to get to know each other well face-to-face.
- **Family:** This group you are bound to through blood and marriage - those whom God has given you through no choice of your own. Some are very easy to love and some are not; but all are a gift to be honored and treated well. We are to honor our parents and love our brothers and sisters – blood and otherwise.
- **Spouse:** This is the most important earthly relationship you choose. Men: don't marry a woman you are not willing to die for. Women: don't marry a man you are not willing to live for. Select a partner with equal values and morals – one who believes as you do. A cord of three is not easily broken. Be yourself and allow your partner to be themselves. Express your needs and desires clearly and pay close attention to what they need. Work on conflicting wants and desires. Have time together and have separate time. Work always on compromise. When you pick a mate, cleave to them – leave all other relationships to a lesser place and cleave to your partner in life.
- **God:** A bond with your Creator/Higher Power is the most important relationship you will make. It can only be accomplished with time and study. God gives guidelines on how to build relationships for us to follow. However, if we don't spend time with Him, if we don't study His word, if we don't follow His rules, we will not have a relationship with Him.

Building Relationships:

The most important aspect of any relationship is trust. With trust you have the ability to share your feelings and needs. Without it, you will always be questioning the relationship. *"Lots of people want to ride with you in the limo, but what you want is someone who will take the bus with you when the limo breaks down"* (Oprah Winfrey).

To build a good relationship, you must spend some time together. You have to listen well, you have to be dependable, and you must honor your word. You must make yourself available when you can if you are needed. You must respect the other person's needs. You must do this with all relationships from **enemies** to **God**. It is important to be interested in the person – not their opinion of you or what they can do for you.

If you have a relationship that is in trouble, don't ignore it. Get to the bottom of what is causing the problem and discuss it so you can come to a mutual understanding if possible. Henry Wadsworth Longfellow made a statement that I think needs to be remembered when we are dealing with others. He said: *"We judge ourselves by what we feel capable of doing, while others judge us by what we have already done."* Others don't always see our potential. They see our past – especially the failures of our past – and we do the same to them.

Be loyal, and in most cases, you will have friends who are also loyal to you. But be loyal even if your friends are not. This reflects on your character, not theirs. Surround yourself with good people. Spend time with people whose morals and values match yours. Always be yourself. The more we live to meet the expectations of someone else, the weaker and shallower and more insecure we become.

Make it a rule to let others know you appreciate them. All people crave praise. Compliment people on the little things. Treating someone as a second-class citizen never gets first-class results. Give credit where credit is due. Praise, like money, stinks if you keep it, but it helps people grow if you spread it around. Have an attitude of "what can I do today to make someone else happy?"

You must know yourself. Have you heard the story of the carrot, the egg, and the tea bag? When you put a carrot in water and boil it, it turns soft; when you do the same with an egg, it becomes hard. But when you put a tea bag in boiling water, it changes the water. Which are you when adversity hits: A carrot? An egg? Or a tea bag?

Getting to know people opens your mind to what is important to you. You learn what behaviors in another make you happy and what behaviors are irritants. (This is an important factor to know before you make a lifetime commitment to a partner.)

Since you cannot achieve great things by yourself, build relationships with people who help you grow, and in turn, be a factor in their growth. The only way to have a friend is to be a friend.

Relationship Questions

What do you like most about yourself?

_____

_____

What would you like to correct about yourself?

_____

_____

Make a list of the most important relationships in your life:

_____   _____

_____   _____

_____   _____

For each relationship, identify one thing you could do to improve that relationship:

_____   _____

_____   _____

_____   _____

What qualities are you looking for in a friend?

_____   _____

_____   _____

_____   _____

Risk Analysis

The more you do, the more you fail;
The more you fail, the more you learn;
The more you learn, the better you get!

When you live to learn, you really learn to live. Failure is either your friend or your enemy, and you get to decide which one it is. If you are determined to learn from your mistakes, you make failure a friend. You will never really know who you are until you test yourself.

If you are not happy with where you are, change. Change is difficult and risky and will not happen until you hurt enough to have to change, learn enough to want to change, or believe enough that you can change. People change when the pain of the present is greater than the fear of the change. To change you need a case of **PTSD:** (**P**ersistence, **T**enacity, **S**elf-discipline, and **D**etermination.) (For more information see the chapter on Change.)

The fuel that makes it possible to conquer new territory is risk, and the nature of risk is that it does not always work out. So you have to have courage to take a risk. Mark Twain says: *"I have lived a long life and had many troubles, most of which never happened."* So stop worrying about the possible negatives and focus on the potential outcome. Don't evaluate the risk based on the fear it generates, but on the probability of the success it brings when the goal is reached. Ironically, the more you risk failure – and actually fail – the greater your chances of success. It is better to try something great and fail than to try nothing and succeed. When there is no hope for the future, there is no power in the present.

Be content but don't be comfortable. Being comfortable is accepting where you are with no desire to change or move. Being content is accepting where you are, expecting a change, working for a change, being solution-oriented, and believing in yourself while maintain a positive attitude. Your attitude will determine your outcome.

Remember, you cannot out-sin God's forgiveness. No matter how important your past, it is not nearly as important as the way you see your future. Say "goodbye" to yesterday. As John Maxwell said: *"Yesterday ended last night."* You cannot be your best today until you let go of the past. Since the past cannot be changed, it is fruitless to carry it around.

You can reach your potential tomorrow, if you dedicate yourself to growth today; but to grow you have to acknowledge both your gifts and your flaws.

Why do some people achieve so much?

- **It is not the family**: Some people from great families fail and some from dysfunctional families succeed.
- **It is not wealth or poverty:** Success has come from both of these environments. **It is not opportunity:** Everyone gets opportunities – it is what they do with these opportunities that matter.
- **It is not morals**: The good, the bad, and the ugly have succeeded at one point or another.
- **It is not hardship or ease:** Both scenarios have produced winners.

The difference between the average and achieving is their perception and response to failure and risk. *". . . there are many ways to be a winner, but there is only one way to be a loser and that is to fail and not look beyond the failure"* (Kyle Rote, Jr.). To fail to learn is failure.

So, how do you fail forward?

You cannot think positively, do nothing, and fail forward. What you have to do is take responsibility for your actions; learn from your mistakes; be open to taking new risks; stay positive; persevere under adversity; and most of all, GET BACK UP! You are a far greater example if you fall and get back up than if you never fell at all. That is the formula. One of the biggest mistakes people make is to take isolated events in their lives, blow them out of proportion, and label them as failures. *"The difference in greatness and mediocrity is often how an individual views a mistake"* (Nelson Boswell). John Maxwell wrote a wonderful book called <u>Failing Forward</u> that I highly recommend.

What failure is NOT!
1. **<u>Failure is not avoidable</u>**: There are no mistakes, only lessons. Lessons are repeated until they are learned; and, if you don't learn the easy lessons, they get harder. You will know you have learned when you change your behavior.

2. **Failure is not an event**: Failure is a process. It is how you deal with the events in your life as they come along.
3. **Failure is not objective**: You are the only one who has the right to declare yourself a failure.
4. **Failure is not the enemy**: Failure is the fertilizer for success. It takes adversity to create success. The person who never makes mistakes takes orders from the one who does. When we give ourselves permission to fail, we open the opportunity to excel.
5. **Failure is not irreversible**: This too will pass. Get up and start over. It does not matter how much milk you spill as long as you don't lose your cow.
6. **Failure is not a stigma**: Mistakes are not permanent markers. They lose their value over time.
7. **Failure is not final**: You will always have an opportunity to go forward and do great things as long as you do not label yourself as a permanent failure.

All roads to achievement lead through the valley of defeat. Failure is simply the price we pay to achieve success. See yourself as God sees you – Royal, Rich, and Righteous. God uses people who are failures because there are no other kinds.

Risk takers see failure as a temporary, isolated event. The greater the feat you desire to achieve, the greater the mental preparation required for overcoming obstacles and persevering over the long haul. *"What distinguishes winners from losers is that winners concentrate at all times on what they CAN do, not on what they cannot do"* (Bob Butera). Gaining personal experience in areas of fear is the key to learning and overcoming future obstacles. A person can fall down many times, but he will not be a failure until he says someone pushed him.

Procrastination is the fertilizer that makes difficulties grow. The man who thinks all day about the catch he missed because of stormy weather ends up wasting time when the sky is clear. Ecclesiastes 11:4 NKJV: *He that observes the wind shall not sow; and he that regards the clouds shall not reap.* Looking at adversity takes away your motivation to take action. If you take action and keep making mistakes, you gain experience.

What holds people in the past?

Past problems either produce a breakdown or a breakthrough; they either make a person bitter or better depending on the attitude toward the problem. You know you are stuck in the past if you are complaining or blaming, rationalizing or excusing, isolating yourself, refusing to forgive, or holding on to bitterness. Your past does not have to discolor your present. Don't let it hold you hostage. Let go of what you cannot change. Every difficulty you face in life is a fork in the road. Let your past experience teach you which path to take. *"Failure is an opportunity to start over again more intelligently"* (John Maxwell).

Not realizing what you want in life is a problem of knowledge. Not pursuing what you want is a problem of motivation. Not achieving what you want is a problem of persistence. *"You can get everything in life you want, if you will help enough other people get what they want"* (Zig Ziglar). Be more concerned with what you can give than what you can get, for giving truly is the highest level of living.

"To achieve your dreams, you must embrace adversity and make failure a regular part of your life. If you are not failing, you are probably not moving forward" (John Maxwell). The only way to get ahead in life is to fail early, fail often, and fail forward. If you have not yet succeeded, it is because you have not yet completed the race.

Risk Analysis

What failures in your life have you refused to release?

_____
_____
_____

If you could redo them, what changes would you make?

_____
_____
_____

What would you like to accomplish in the future?

_____
_____
_____

What are you afraid of?

_____
_____
_____

Facing our fears and putting them on paper will often reduce the effect they have on us.

Self-Discipline
***The price of discipline is always
less than the pain of regret!***

Self-discipline is the art of getting yourself to do, or not do, something even when your emotions or body are telling you to do the opposite. Moods, appetite, and passions are powerful forces to go against. It takes **courage**. You know you are self-disciplined when you reach the point where you make a decision and follow through on it. If you are self-disciplined, you can overcome any addiction, lose any amount of weight, and eliminate procrastination, disorder and ignorance.

However, it takes self-discipline to become self-disciplined. Stephen Covey says: To improve, *"we must start from where we are – not from where we should be, or where someone else is, or even where someone else thinks we are"* (or thinks we should be). Look at any failure, as John Maxwell does, as an opportunity to start again more intelligently. If your goal is to be self-disciplined, then you must make a conscious **effort** toward that end. You have to build one step at a time – just as you would in a weight room. If you want an example of how to become self-disciplined, read Benjamin Franklin's Autobiography. List virtues that are important to you and follow his plan. As you go through this process, don't compare yourself with others. It never helps.

In *Benjamin Franklin's Autobiography*, pages 104-107, he gives us detailed information on how he changed his life by deciding what virtues he wanted to acquire and then creating a system that allowed him to measure his progress toward that goal.

He first listed the virtue, defined it for himself, and then set up a chart to track his progress. He chose to tackle one virtue at a time on a chart with seven columns (to represent each day of the week). At the top of the chart would be the virtue he was working on that week and a definition of the virtue. Down the left side of the page would be one word each for all of the virtues he intended to work on.

For one week he would concentrate only on the titled virtue. He would make a mark in the daily column of each fault he committed that day, with a goal of having no marks in the row for the virtue he was concentrating on. The next week, he would go to the next virtue and work on that one – not forgetting the first, just not giving it the primary focus. When all of his virtues were covered once, he would start over. This was a lifetime process for him, as it should be for each of us.

As an example, this is the list of Benjamin Franklin's 13 virtues and his definitions as recorded in his autobiography:

1. **Temperance**: Eat not to dullness; drink not to elevation.
2. **Silence**: Speak not but what may benefit others or yourself; avoid trifling conversation.
3. **Order**: Let all your things have their places; let each part of your business have its time.
4. **Resolution**: Resolve to perform what you ought; perform without fail what you resolve.
5. **Frugality**: Make no expense but to do good to others or yourself; that is, waste nothing.
6. **Industry**: Lose no time; be always employed in something useful; cut off all unnecessary actions.
7. **Sincerity**: Use no hurtful deceit; think innocently and justly; and if you speak, speak accordingly.
8. **Justice**: Wrong none by doing injuries or omitting the benefits that are your duty.
9. **Moderation**: Avoid extremes; forbear resenting injuries, so much as you think they deserve.
10. **Cleanliness**: Tolerate no un-cleanliness in body, clothes, or habitation.
11. **Tranquility**: Be not disturbed by trifles or at accidents common or unavoidable.
12. **Chastity**: (Apparently no explanation is needed here as Mr. Franklin did not give one.)
13. **Humility**: Imitate Jesus and Socrates.

Self-discipline requires that you act on what you think rather than what you feel. Pick your own list of virtues and act on them. (Decide what is best and do it.) Know what is important to you. You cannot succeed without **commitment** – commitment to yourself and to others. Don't say you will do something until you know you will.

Leadership is not possible without self-discipline. YOU are the first person you lead. *"In the beginning, self-discipline is the choice of achieving what you really want by doing the things you really don't want to do. In the end, self-discipline becomes the choice of achieving what you really want by doing the things you now want to do"* (John Maxwell). Once you see the positive results of a behavior, you create a desire to do even the tasks you don't like in order to get the results you want. Harry Truman did a study of great men to determine what they considered was their first great victory. In every case, the response was "self-discipline."

Be careful how you talk to yourself. Your first step in self-discipline is to **control** what you think and say to yourself. Most people do not take the time to think about what they are thinking about. They allow random thoughts to flow through their head without stopping to analyze their benefit or detriment. Self-talk can be harmful, but it can be very helpful if you control the direction it takes and apply some of the self-image principles you have learned.

One of the main characteristics of self-discipline is the ability to forego instant gratification and pleasure in favor of some greater gain or more satisfying result – even though it requires time and effort.

HOW TO DEVELOP SELF-DISCIPLINE:

Create new habits to replace the old. For example:
- Find new words to express your frustrations – eliminate the poor language even in your head.
- Set an earlier time to rise and go to bed to ensure you get enough sleep.
- Change a sweet or salty snack for a piece of fruit or a protein.

Schedule your tasks for a particular time of day: Make a list of all the things you need to do. Schedule them and do them when you have them scheduled.

- Start every day with a meditation/devotion.
- Check your email at specific times rather than all day long.
- Pick a specific time or day to clean your space.

- Set a time to read every day (at least 15 minutes) on a topic that will educate you in an area you want to progress.

KNOW YOURSELF:

To be self-disciplined, it is important to know yourself. How do you increase your knowledge of yourself? What plan do you have in place for your continued education?

There are many helpful books in this area. Among my favorites are the Florence Littauer *Personality Plus* books, where you can learn not only how and why you react as you do but also why others react to you the way they do. Also, check out the leadership and teamwork books by John Maxwell which direct you in character development and leadership abilities.

Your **first** self-discipline habit should be to develop a habit of reading for at least 15 minutes every day on some subject that will improve your productivity and your leadership abilities. That is called investing your time rather than spending it.

Take an inventory of yourself. How do you handle stressful situations? Do you have effective time-management skills? Do you promote good relationships and alliances? Are your personal, family, and business goals written down? Do you delegate well? Do you know the direction you want to go? Do you have a mission statement for your life?

Personal Mission Statement:

A personal mission statement is a concise description of what you want to be and what you would like to accomplish in certain areas of your life. It is not where you have been or where you are. Make it simple and brief. It should be positive, affirming, compelling, and inspirational. It should excite you and build your character. It should move you closer to your long-term vision.

The difference in a mission statement and a vision statement is that the mission statement is more immediate and may change as you grow. A vision statement tends to focus on the long-range. It is what you want to be remembered for when your life is over. A mission statement shows you an idealized description of your ultimate destination and the vision statement shows your chosen path to get there. Once you know your purpose, how you are going to help others, you can then determine your mission for your life. Keep it positive.

To create a mission statement, you need to identify your talents, your positive personality traits, your beliefs, and your values. Write them down. Are you funny? Nurturing? Caring? Bubbly? Generous? Gentle? Encouraging? Motivational? Optimistic? Inspiring? A good listener? A great friend? What are your beliefs and values? What is important to you? What are you not willing to compromise?

An example of a formula to produce a mission statement is as follows: "My mission is to use my (talent and passion) and (my personality traits) so that (I can accomplish my beliefs/values)." You fill in the blanks. As an example: "My mission is to use my passion for the environment and my optimistic personality to stir people into action so that I can help protect the earth." Once you determine your mission, write it down, memorize it, and state it daily to keep you on track. Keep it simple, clear and brief. Your mission statement may change as you grow and your circumstances change.

Set Your Mission Statement:

To set your mission statement, you need to know where you want to go in life. The power to achieve the life of your dreams is in your hands – and the first step to achieving it is to identify it. Most people do not get what they want out of life because they do not know what they want from life. Use the following questions to help you create your own personal mission statement:

1. Who do you know (or know of) that is doing what you like to do and what are they doing?
   _____
   _____

2. How do you define success?
   _____
   _____

3. Who do you know (or know of) that you feel is leading a successful life according to your definition of success?
   _____
   _____

Let's think about the important people in your life. Pick your top three and list these people in order of importance from one to five (5): (If they are of equal importance, just list them.)

1. _____

2. _____

3. _____

What do you respect the most about each person?

1. _____

2. _____

3. _____

What main trait will you remember them for?

1. _____

2. _____

3. _____

Of the traits above, which three are the most important to you? Which ones do you want to be remembered for?

_____

_____

_____

Now that you know the type of person you want to become, write out your mission in paragraph form:

_____

_____

_____

You can be confident that if honesty, dependability, encouragement, or thoughtfulness is important to you, these traits are also important to those you care about.

My **mission** statement is as follows: *I am a child of God and a sister of Christ, living a life my children would be proud to emulate, by helping people to help themselves so they, in turn, can help others.*

Here is my **vision** statement: *I want to be remembered as a motivator and encourager for everyone I meet.*

In conclusion, we know that self-discipline takes courage, effort, commitment, and control. As you know, deciding what to **BE** is more important than deciding what to **DO**. Until we know what we want to be, what we do will be a waste of time.

Another reason for being self-disciplined is to teach others how to be. You will find attached a chart for you to use in attaining the characteristics that are important to you. Feel free to make copies of this form for each virtue you select to work on.

Virtue: _____
Definition: _____

Virtue	Sun	Mon	Tue	Wed	Thu	Fri	Sat

Self-Perception:
How we see ourselves
*"It is not that we fear the place of darkness,
but that we don't think we are worth the effort
to find the place of light."*
Hugh Prather

From the day we are born until the day we die, we will be bombarded with other people's opinions of who we are, who we should be, or who they think we should be. But to be perfectly honest, other people's opinions of us are none of our business. Why do we worry about what others think of us? Do we have more confidence in their opinion than we do in our own? The only opinion of you that counts is that of your Creator; for it is only the manufacturer that knows how the product is supposed to work.

One of the biggest challenges all of us face is allowing someone else's opinion of us to define our own image. Self-esteem is how you feel about yourself – are you worthy to be loved? What you think of yourself today may be a result of what a parent, spouse, teacher, boss, co-worker, or friend thought of you in the past. Robert Schuller once said, *"I am not who I think I am. I am not who you think I am. I am who I think you think I am."* Nothing is more stabilizing than a healthy sense of loving one's self. Parents may die, spouses may leave, friends may fail, but the relationship we build with ourselves will last a lifetime. When we feel good about ourselves, we don't need validation from anyone else. *"A man cannot be comfortable without his own approval"* (Mark Twain).

If you add up all you have and subtract all you owe, you will know your self-worth in dollars. If you look in the mirror and note what you are wearing and how you have cleaned up, you will see your self-image from the vision. But if you want to evaluate your self-esteem (or your self-perception), you must go deep inside yourself; and only you and your God can determine the value. If you think you are weird, Johnny Depp says that is OK. *"I think everybody is weird. We should all celebrate our individuality and not be embarrassed or ashamed of it."*

Our self-perception determines our behavior. You have to love who you are so you can give the respect you deserve to receive – whether you receive it or not. Until you value yourself, you will not value your time. Until you value your time, you will not do anything with it. If we think we are inadequate, we will act inadequate. If we think we are OK, we will act OK. Our success and happiness are determined by our thinking. Change the way we think, and we change our outcome. Take a good look at yourself and change what you don't like.

Don't compare yourself with others. Comparisons lead to feelings of inferiority or superiority – but seldom do they produce emotional health. Comparing yourself with someone else will only keep you stuck. You cannot compare an alligator with a rock. They have nothing in common. You cannot even compare an apple with an orange; for, even if they are both fruits, they are unique fruits. Humility does not mean groveling or feeling inferior or worthless, nor does it imply disliking oneself. If you feel you are worthless, either your feelings are liars or God is. Which one do you think is most reliable? When we deny we have value, we are, in essence, being too proud to accept the value that has been put in us. True humility is seeing ourselves and accepting ourselves as God sees us and accepts us. Humility is not thinking less of yourself, it is thinking of yourself less often. *"Let everyone be sure that he is doing his very best, for then he will have the personal satisfaction of work well done and won't need to compare himself with someone else"* (Galatians 6:4).

Not liking yourself pulls you down. It is like going through life with your parking brakes on. Feeling good about yourself is not a selfish act. It is simply accepting the stewardship given to you of the gifts you have to help others. It is never too late to become what you should be. When you look in the mirror, what do you see: a failure, a stumbling block, a mess? Or do you see a person with potential, a kind heart, a good mind, talented and with ability? It is a choice. (No matter how important your past, it is not nearly as important as the way you see your future.) It is what you see in your future that will pull you to your full potential.

You cannot go back and make a new start, but you can go forward and create a new end. Don't make excuses for the past. God created the past so we would have a place to bury our mistakes. Though we need to acknowledge wrongs to right them, we do not need to carry them into the future with us. Failures are simply learning-stones to success. Even though there are no excuses for bad behavior, we have to accept those behaviors, learn from them, and move forward. *"Don't ask God to guide your footsteps if you are not willing to move your feet"* (Anonymous).

Learn from the Past
Plan for the Future
Live in the Present

Yesterday is history
Tomorrow is a mystery
Today is a gift –
That's why it is called the present!

Since we did not create ourselves, we do not need to look to ourselves to fix ourselves. That is not our job. When we have a problem with our car, we take it to the mechanic. Ask help from your Maker. When we improve how we feel about ourselves, we help other people improve also. If it is alright for you to like you, that means it is also OK for others to like themselves.

Changing the way you see yourself also changes the way you see others, for what we see in others is a mirror of what we see in ourselves. We initially can only see qualities we had, have, or are in the process of developing. To change your self-esteem, change your vocabulary. Don't use the word "can't" to describe your abilities. Change it to "I don't want to" or "I don't choose to," or even "I haven't learned that yet." Personal growth begins when we are willing to change the words we use to describe our own talents and abilities, and start to define what we are capable of doing and are willing to learn. Keep your expectations positive, for you will prevent yourself from wanting what you think you cannot have.

To take the first step on your road to a better self-perception, start with self-talk. Research has shown that for every minute of negative, berating self-talk it takes ten minutes of positive thought too. On average, most children receive 148,000 negative comments by the time they are eighteen. No wonder so many of us have very low self-esteem. What a waste of time! We have to reverse these messages to be sure they are not passed down to the next generation. Keep a tight grip on your actions and words for *"you cannot un-see what you have seen or un-do what you have done"* (Tyrone Maddox). Look at yourself as a gift God has given this world – just waiting to be unwrapped. Your value will be determined by the service you are willing to give.

Your self-esteem affects every aspect of your life: Spiritual (how you feel about God), Mental (how you think about things), Physical (how you take care of yourself), Family (how value your relationship), Social (how you relate to others), Financial (how you manage your money), and Career (how you grow in your job or business). How you feel about yourself should have nothing to do with your income, your reputation, your occupation, your race, your clothes, religion, or education. It does not have anything to do with your ethnic background, your possessions, your sex, your car, or your zip code. It has everything to do with admitting you have talents, determining what those talents are, and then using them.

You can only give to others what you have within yourself to give. Therefore, it is very important that you love who and what you are so you can give back the respect you need and want to receive.

- **How do you feel about your mind?** Are you continuously learning? If you are not learning, you are not growing.
- **How do you feel about your body?** Do you exercise and take care of yourself? Without exercise, you will not have the energy to do all you need to do.
- **How do you feel about your thoughts?** Are you careful to maintain a positive mind-set? How you think will determine what you become. You will always believe what you tell yourself more than you will even believe an expert. You will never rise above the image you have of yourself in your mind.
- **How do you feel about your appearance?** Do you get cleaned up every day whether you are going anywhere or not? We perform better and feel better when we are ready for whatever comes our way.
- **How do you feel about your talents?** Do you know you have talents? Do you use your abilities to help others? This is your reason for living, your purpose in life. It is why God put you here in the first place.

Never compare yourself with another human. You are fearfully, wonderfully, and uniquely made. You are not comparable. Don't confuse self-esteem with how you look or what you have. That is not what is important. Don't pretend. *"Don't get lost in the artificial image of who you are trying to project yourself to be"* (Jay Rifenbary). Believe in yourself. Acknowledge who you are. Respect yourself. Don't let fear control you. Let go of self-doubt. What is inside of you is all that can come out. The way you change your self-image is to get to know yourself. Loving yourself is not self-centeredness; it is Godliness. It is following the rules. Self-esteem does not mean "I", "me", or "my". It is not self-centered; it is self-improving.

Be willing to learn and change the way you feel about yourself and live for today. We learn from parents, siblings, spouses, teachers, friends, books, television, and society. Much of what we learn is before we are of an age to discern if it is true or not. If taught incorrectly, it can destroy a life.

It is so much more difficult to unlearn than to learn. Unlearning is a process of changing the way you see things. Every hope, wish, desire, and dream is birthed in your imagination. Denis Kimbro says, *"You cannot think your way into acting positively, but you can act your way into thinking positively."* Change the way you act. Put a smile on your face and good thoughts in your mind. Act like you like you.

Self-evaluation is made up of four basic areas:

1. Confidence – how much faith do we have in our abilities
2. Appearance – how well do we take care of ourselves
3. Relationships – how we treat God, family, and friends
4. Values – what is important to us

A person's self-esteem is obvious from the way they treat others. Self-esteem begins at birth and either improves or diminishes by the treatment we receive and the reaction we have to that treatment. We can improve the way we see ourselves by the choices we make, and we can improve the self-esteem of another by the way we treat them. While you can't do anything about your ancestors, you can influence your descendants greatly. What will it take to make you do what you need to do to change your self-perception? How far down must you go to make you look up? What is the turning point for you? You cannot change the events of the past, but you can change the choices of the future.

One result of a negative impression is a fear of failure. Fear of failure comes from excessive criticism. Criticism causes us to not take risks, and without risk not much happens. The more intact your self-esteem, the less fear you have and the greater risk you are willing to take. Mark Twain says: *"Twenty years from now, you will be more disappointed in the things you did not do than by the things you did do."* If you believe you have a chance of getting what you want from life, you are far more willing to work for it.

A second result of a negative self-evaluation is a fear of rejection; and fear of rejection comes from conditional love. Conditional love is based on performance, and all performance is subject to error. Unconditional love is based on caring about the person regardless of performance. Unconditional love is the greatest gift we can receive or give. If you choose to please someone, do it because you want to not because you feel you have to. When you do what is correct for you, and it does not hurt anyone else, you have done what is best for both.

We cannot change what has happened to us in the past. What is done is done and cannot be undone. All we can do is prepare for the future and learn and grow from our experiences. There will be mistakes from us and other, and it will be up to us to correct our errors. But with effort and attention, we can grow and change our opinion of ourselves. Preparation always promotes an awareness of self and the world as it is, not as we wish it to be. Self-awareness always enhances strength and resilience. As the samurai put it, *"It is the journey that makes the warrior."* To face the fact that we need to change is the first step. However, unless we actually take the step, nothing changes.

Identify what you love about yourself. Identify your values and talents. When you recognize your values, your confidence will not be shaken when faced with societies demands on you to do as others want you to do. Their choice will not determine your worthiness. The rejection we feel from others is often a result of how we feel about ourselves, for **what we see in others is often a mirror of what we see in ourselves.** It is difficult to feel good about yourself if you violate your values. It is important to always "do the right thing" – to be honest and sincere in all that we do. Do everything to the best of your ability.

Enjoy, recognize and reward the little successes along the way. Good self-esteem creates energy, enthusiasm, and excitement. Don't live your life based on what others expect of you. Treat others with respect, kindness, love, and sincerity. Meet people at their need. If you want to feel good about yourself, help others feel good about themselves. When you plant a seed of kindness, it will come back to you – whether it comes from the person you planted it in or someone else, you will get it back. You will always reap what you sow.

Put yourself on a continuing education program so you can feel more confident in yourself. Use your talents, gifts, and skills. Self-perception is a gradual process. Something you work on for a lifetime. You are not your past behavior. Behaviors change. Learn from them and move forward. Get in touch with yourself. Know what you are good at; know what makes you happy; know who you want to be; and know what is important to you. Do everything you do to the best of your ability, so you can feel good about yourself and reward yourself along the way. *"As you think and behave, so shall you become."* (Lou Holtz)

Use all your senses to create an image of yourself. Then **see** it, **write** it, **read** it, **say** it, and **act** it, so you can **taste** it!

"Some people are going to like me, some people are not. So, I might as well be me; because then I know that the people who like me, like ME!"

(Prather)

"When one door closes, another opens; but, we often look so regretfully upon the closed door that we don't see the one that has opened for us."

(Alexander Graham Bell)

Self-Perception: How you see yourself

What is the one thing you like the most about yourself?

_____

_____

What do you value the most about yourself?

_____

_____

What is one thing you need to change to make you feel better about yourself?

_____

_____

What is one thing you could do today to help someone else feel better about themselves?

_____

_____

Write a positive description of **YOU**.

_____

_____

Self-Talk

"There is no greater path you can walk, no greater goal you can achieve, and no greater purpose you can find than to live up to the promise you were born to fulfill."
(Shad Helmsetter)

Every action you take comes from a thought you have. Some thoughts are conscious and some are sub-conscious. Your heart pumps and your digestive system works without your conscious knowledge of what is taking place. But when you take any action, it is a result of your conscious thoughts derived from your life experiences (whether you remember them or not). Your body is fearfully and wonderfully made and is directed by a brain that can out-perform any computer. But just like a computer, what you put into your brain is what comes out in actions.

Let's review basically how the brain works:

- Every event, word, and thought experienced is recorded in the mind at least temporarily.
- The brain reacts to the strongest messages it receives.
- The sub-conscious mind will accept what you feed it; and the more emotion you give it when you feed it, the more permanent the thought will be.
- When positive, uplifting things are sent to the brain, it wires the neural network in the **left prefrontal cortex** of the brain, which is the center that helps you deal with problems.
- When negative things go in, the **right lobe**, which is the area that triggers a fight or flight mode of escape, is reprogrammed.
- The brain continuously rewrites itself throughout life and we are constantly reprogramming it.

Statistics tell us that even when a child is raised in a relatively positive home, by the time they are 18 years old they have heard more than 60 times as many version of the word "NO" than "YES". This means we are constantly programming for a way of escape (as opposed to a way to face the challenge). Some of those negatives can and should carry with us to adult hood: "Don't cross the street without looking both ways." Some are reserved until we reach the age of making our own decisions: "Don't talk to strangers." But a vast majority of them are relegated to the sub-conscious mind and are, in fact, untruths that we should replace with positive thoughts. Our thoughts are controlled by the programs we have spent a lifetime storing in our sub-conscious mind.

The sub-conscious mind has no way of determining what is true and what is false. It simply holds on to the things that are most often repeated; and the more emotion the statements are given, the harder the sub-conscious holds on to them. As a result, if we have been told from an early age (and with great force) that our life should or should not take a certain direction, the mind will push us in that direction - even if the direction is wrong. The biggest challenge with this is that the ones giving direction are often people who want what they think is best for us. If they are wrong, we are left with reprogramming our minds.

As serious a challenge as it is for someone else to mislead us, it is even more difficult when we do it ourselves; for we will always believe what we tell ourselves before we will believe what anyone else tells us. Og Mandino said, *"No one in life has deceived me as much as I have. The most harmful enemy I have is me."* Unfortunately, what we tell ourselves is often reflective of what we have been told. Science says we have over 6,000 thoughts a day and most of them are automatic without our even realizing we are having them. After absorbing all the statements we have collected from childhood, we start to believe things that are not true and act on them. If we have been told often enough that we are "not good at" or "not smart enough" or "not capable" or "too sensitive" or any other negative, we hold ourselves back from accomplishing whatever it is we would like to go after. So, what is your self-talk doing to you? Is it holding you up or is it letting you down?

Self-talk is the ongoing message you are feeding yourself about yourself. When you talk to yourself, you are planning your future. You are directing your success or failure, your happiness or depression, based on your thoughts of plenty or of fear and failure. Everything you do is affected directly or indirectly by your attitude. Attitude is formed in our minds through our thoughts. Attitude affects our feelings and feelings then reinforce thoughts. Thoughts lead to our actions, which lead to success or failure based on what we have told ourselves. Our thoughts create our attitude, our attitude creates our feelings, our feelings determine our actions, and our actions produce results. The mind will do for us what we tell it to do the most.

The key to all management (the management of others, of resources, or of the future) is self-management; and self-management comes from self-talk. Talk to yourself as if speaking to someone you love. Be your own best friend. Be kind to you. Be caring, strong, demanding, and determined. That is how God made you, and you can do all things through Him. Build yourself up on the inside, for the more successful you are on the inside, the more successful you automatically become on the outside. Self-talk is full of value judgments, but not always facts. When you put yourself down, you are attacking your own best ally – the one person whose support you cannot succeed without.

Success is all about what you think. So when you are talking to yourself, follow the rules;

1. You are unique, so don't compare yourself with anyone other than your creator.
2. Don't blame or complain. Just look at the facts. Wherever you are, you can improve.
3. Focus on what you want from life and be willing to go after it.
4. Respect yourself. Don't look at your mistakes as a personal failure, just as feedback for improvement.
5. If you need help, get help.
6. Be grateful for ALL things (1 Thessalonians 5: 18), for you are exactly where you are suppose to be.
7. Use your self-talk to learn and grow.

"Many intelligent adults...are restrained in thoughts, actions and results. They never move further than the boundaries of their self-imposed limitations." (John Maxwell, The Winning Attitude, pg. 79) Self-imposed limitations come from self-talk. When you treat yourself with respect, patience, and kindness (as you would anyone else), you motivate yourself with confidence to keep going and not give up. Cruelty will not motivate you. What you put into your mind is what will push you to a better life.

Good self-talk has to be cultivated. We live in a world where negative thoughts come more naturally – probably because of all those NOs we heard growing up. But when you create positive self-talk you eliminate unnecessary suffering on your part and on the part of those who care about you. To love our neighbor as ourselves, we have to love our self first.

"Usually negative opinions about us by others do not bother us unless they echo something we have also been saying to ourselves. We all have a constant, flowing stream of ideas running through our minds that make up who we think we

are and how we feel about ourselves. Some of it is good and some of it is bad; some of it is true and some of it is not. Throughout life, people are going to be critical. We are sometimes too. If someone else's opinion of you makes you feel bad about you, know that the reason their words have power is because you said them first in your mind. Your words are what need to be analyzed. Maybe there is some truth you need to acknowledge and work on, or maybe it is a lie you need to ignore – or maybe it is a little of both." (Zach Whitzel)

Work on your self-talk so that your words paint a picture of what you want your life to look like. Putting yourself down with negative self-talk works to your disadvantage. Anytime you talk to yourself, you are reinforcing your opinion of you. And any time you talk to someone else about you, you are doing the same. To our subconscious mind, a problem is only as bad as we perceive it to be. If we face our challenges with a positive self-talk, the problem is reduced and the brain starts working on a solution.

Make a conscious effort to think about what you are thinking about; and if you discover that your self-talk is more negative than positive, create new habits to turn it around. Evaluate your self-talk. How do you respond when you burn the toast or remember something you forgot to do? How do you react when you remember something you should not have done? Do you immediately begin to beat yourself up? Would you do that to a friend? If so, you have some changes to make.

What we tell ourselves about our problems will determine the actions we take to solve them. We can only do what we believe we can do. Evaluating what you tell yourself will reveal who or what is controlling your life. What causes you discomfort? What memories are causing you to go negative when faced with a challenge? What things on the outside are affecting the way you think? Are you judging yourself by someone else's opinion of you? Are you doing things because you have been led to believe you have to or to satisfy someone else's desires for you? Have the challenges of your youth led you to believe you cannot succeed in the future?

Negative self-talk includes looking for what won't work, over focusing on fears, looking for faults and flaws, and seeing problems instead of challenges. Negative self-talk sets you up for failure. It becomes a habit if you don't control it. It is a learned habit from your past experiences and the negative thoughts that have been planted in your mind from others and from yourself. But, since it is a learned habit, it can be changed. This is God's recommendation:

*"Finally, brethren, whatsoever **things** are true, whatsoever **things** are honest, whatsoever **things** are just, whatsoever **things** are pure, whatsoever **things** are lovely, whatsoever **things** are of good report; if there be any virtue, and if there be any praise, **think on these things**."*
(Philippians 4:8)

Neuroplasticity refers to the brain's ability to form new networks based on new information. In other words, your brain is always learning. What you experience, what you think, and what you say changes the connections in your brain. Since your sub-conscious retains what it is fed most often, repetition of positive self-talk will reprogram your mind. You will believe things about yourself that you tell yourself most often. So, if you find that you are stuck in the trap of negative self-talk, here are a few things you can do to fix it:

- Negative self-talk was created over time, but it does not take as much time to reprogram. It usually takes a few weeks of repeated and reinforced positive self-talk to change the way you think.
- Each time you catch yourself being negative, change the thought. There is no thought that may have been negative in the past that cannot be turned around and be re-worded in a positive direction.
- Be Persistent, Tenacious, Self-disciplined, and Determined (PTSD) to change your thought patterns.

You have not lost the potential you were born with. No one is born to fail. It has just been buried under the negative programming. *"Be transformed by the renewing of your mind"* (Romans 12:2) A rainy day is not a bad day. A mistake is not a failure unless you don't get back up. A skinned knee is not a fatal event. Don't let the dreams of your youth fade. What we perceive and what we accept is an important part of what we will become. We are responsible for what we allow in our minds.

"A noble and Godlike character is not a thing of favor or chance, but is the natural result of continued effort in right thinking, the effect of long-cherished association with Godlike thoughts." (Ken Blanchard)

Self-Talk

What topic do you find yourself talking to yourself about most often?

_____

_____

What is your fondest memory in life?

_____

_____

What saying can you plant in your mind to remind you to shift your thinking to something positive when the negative thoughts come?

_____

_____

What is one thought you have that you know is holding you back from your full potential? Re-write that thought to a positive and memorize it.

_____

_____

_____

_____

Success Principles

"How do you get from where you are
to where you want to be?"
(Jack Canfield)

You are in the best position you will ever be in to succeed because you are right where God has allowed you to be (Jeremiah 29:11). He put you here to prosper you.

It is true that where we are is determined by the choices we made in the past, but the direction those choices lead us to is directed by a much higher power. We are not in control; we just think we are. This world has a set of rules: some physical (like gravity), and some Spiritual (like "thou shalt not"). The difference is the Spiritual rewards or consequences do not always come immediately. They require patience, persistence, and perspiration. Even some of the negative results can be reversed with effort.

Jack Canfield wrote a book, **Success Principles**, which outlines the steps to success in business. However, Jack Canfield's success principles apply not only to business, but also to life. He says, to be successful in any endeavor, it is necessary to take 100% responsibility for our actions and our thoughts. Until we stop blaming others, we cannot move forward and we cannot clarify for ourselves what our purpose in life is. To move forward, we have to decide what we want out of life.

Once we identify what we want, we can set goals to attain it. But to attain those goals, we must be able to measure our success. We have to break the goals down to attainable parts. We must convince ourselves through positive self-talk and visualization that this purpose can be accomplished. You don't have to do it alone. All of this will be much easier with an accountability partner.

Start now doing something every day that will lead you toward accomplishing your goals. Don't quit! Once you know what you need to do, do whatever it takes. Be willing to ask for what you need. Move forward even if you are afraid. Study, research, learn, and improve.

- You will make lots of mistakes – that is what it takes to learn.
- You will have fear – that comes with any new venture.
- You will want to quit, because change is hard. Procrastination will be a big temptation.

To move forward, you have to clean up the things in your life that are incomplete; any undone projects, any unfinished business. Know that you are given talents, that you have abilities, and that you are fearfully and wonderfully made. Work on your belief in yourself and your Creator.

Look at the habits you have created in your life and replace poor habits with good one. This is not easy, but it is necessary. One way to change is to learn and the easiest way to learn is to read or listen to training tapes. Make it a habit to read 10 pages a day and you will finish a 300-page book every month. Choose what you read carefully, for you are responsible for what you put into your mind.

Learn to say "no" to any activity that takes you away from your goals. Don't allow yourself to be distracted. If you find it difficult to stay focused, find a mentor or hire a coach. Control your time so it is spent where it is important to you; with your Creator, yourself, your family, and your job.

Don't lose those who are special to you in the process of growing; plan time with them on a daily, weekly, or monthly basis depending on the relationship. Schedule a vacation once a year where the important people in your life can have your full attention; and you will all have something to look forward to as you work toward completing your goals.

Work on getting your money in order: give 10%, save 10%, and live on 80%. Stop any impulse buying. Cut back on frivolous spending. Become more valuable at your job by going the extra mile or at your business by giving more excellent service.

Success principles are the same for life and for business. It is what you have to do to go to the next level. *"You will never change your life until you change something you do daily. The secret to your success is found in your daily routine"* John Maxwell.

Obviously, the first step in any endeavor is to know where you want to go and when you want to get there. There may be many alternative routes, but only one ideal destination.

What is that destination for you?

Make sure your goal is worth reaching. Be sure the reward for attaining it is what you want. Be sure it is worthy enough to make you fight for it, and exciting enough to keep you interested. If you need help determining what you want in life, find someone you trust and talk it out. It is inside of you.

Motivation comes from within. If it does not, any distraction will take you off course. It is up to you to maintain your focus. One-day-at-a-time is all you get. So even though you focus on the future, you work in the present.

Jack Canfield's Principles for Success

* Take 100% responsibility for your actions
* Clarify your purpose in life
* Decide what you want out of life
* Set measurable goals and break them down to doable parts
* Create affirmations (positive self-talk)
* Visualize where you want to end up
* Get an accountability partner
* Do something every day to move you forward
* Do whatever it takes to get the job done
* Ask for what you need
* Work even if you are afraid – have no fear
* Learn something new every day
* Clean up any incompletes
* Work on your belief
* Replace poor habits with good
* Read and listen to training tapes
* Say no to distractions
* Find a mentor or coach
* Schedule a vacation

Success Principles

What is one habit you know you need to break?

_____

What positive advice could you give yourself every day to move you forward?

_____

_____

What is one thing you could do today that would make your tomorrow better?

_____

What is one goal you could accomplish that would increase your self-worth?

_____

Identify one book you could read that would help you reach your goals.

_____

Identify one person in your life that would be a good mentor for you.

_____

What is one expense you could eliminate to improve your financial situation?

_____

Time Management

"Unless you are consistently making the opportunity to accomplish things that are important or meaningful to you, being better organized will only fill up your time and make you more frustrated."
John Maxwell

The absence of time management leads to an unnecessary level of stress. Doing a better job of managing your time is meaningless unless you are managing it to accomplish those things that are most important to you. You know you need to work on time management if:

- You have to rush at the last minute to meet deadlines.
- You find yourself double-booked for appointments (when you did not need to be).
- You conduct (or attend) meetings that achieve nothing.
- Your days seem to slip by unproductively.
- You find yourself constantly fighting one crisis after another.
- You get to the end of the day and feel you have accomplished nothing.

The greater your responsibility, the greater is your need for an organized, timely schedule. Managing your time is *"… a tool for systematic ordering of your influence on events"* (Gerald M. Blair).

Managing your personal time allows you to control your workload and eliminate wasted time. It allows you to put first things first and it allows you to:

- Plan each day efficiently.

- Plan each week effectively.

- Plan each month productively.

- Have more fun.

If you have ever been on a weight-loss program, you know that one of the first tips you are given is to write down everything that you eat. It is amazing how much control you exert over yourself when you are forced to acknowledge just what you are putting into your mouth. Time Management works the same way. The first step toward managing time is to record exactly what you do every day for one week. Record time in fifteen-minute segments, starting with the time you get up and ending with the time you go to bed. (If you are not scheduling for the amount of sleep you need, this is the first correction you need to make in your time management.) Your mind does not work at its best without adequate rest.

There are times in our lives when we feel we are completely out of control. When this happens, it is important to step back and evaluate the situation. The only thing you completely control is you. Everything else is partial control at best. Now that you know how you spend your time, you might find it helpful to list the events of your week by activity and then grade them as to the degree of control you feel you have over them. You will find an example on the next page.

Notice in this example that "traffic" is given some level of control. You know when the peak travel times are, and you can avoid them to some extent. Note also that you have total control over when you get up in the morning and a great deal of control over what you choose to eat for each meal.

The other thing that is totally within your control is your reaction to the events around you. *"What is important is not that there are uncontrollable events in our lives, but how we respond to them"* (Hyrum W. Smith). Meetings are often controlled by who is calling the meeting. If it is for a boss or customer, you want to be available; but the timing may not always be the best. If you are calling a meeting with your friends/family, you have more (if not complete) control.

The next step is to use this information to control what you can control and to accept what you cannot (and to recognize the difference). This step alone will greatly reduce your level of stress. Look at each activity and see how much it is worth to you. Where did it fall on your list of priorities? List your activities one more time; this time in order of importance to you.

You may be surprised to find that some of the activities that are most important to you do not show up on your list you made from your daily activities – like spending time with your God, family, and friends, reading a book, exercising, playing, etc. Often the most important things DO NOT get done.

When the need is great enough, we control all kinds of events that we normally believed we could not control. The only difference is our need to control them. For example, according to several time-management studies, the average person works 47 hours a week and the average millionaire works about 54 hours each week – that is only a seven hour difference. Think about this. If you could be assured by working an additional seven hours a week that you would be a millionaire, would you find the extra seven hours? Some of you would and some of you wouldn't, but all of you could by managing your time better.

Activity Control Chart (Sample)

List each activity and determine your level of control over the event.

5 would equal total control and **0** would equal no control.

Activity	Control Level
Time I get up in the morning	5
What I eat for breakfast	4
Traffic to work	2
Telephone interruptions	3
Boss/Customer interruptions	2
Friend/Family interruptions	4
How I react to a bad situation	5
Meetings with friends/family	3
Meetings with boss/customers	2
What to eat for lunch	4
Travel time	2
Family emergencies	0

Don't misunderstand. Money is not the issue here. You could replace money with a goal of your own. Would you be willing to plan and organize your time to create an additional seven hours a week to spend with the most important people in your life or to add a few hours of sleep so you could function better? Would you find a few hours to read, walk, swim, or listen to music?

It is important to recognize that we have the same amount of time today as we will have tomorrow or ten years from now. There will NEVER be more time. We all have 24 hours (or 1,440 minutes) a day. Time is a challenge. You cannot save it or return it; you can only invest it or spend it. So, we need to plan our time so that we get the best return on our investment. Don't ever tell yourself (or anyone else) that you don't have time to do something. Be honest with yourself and say (to yourself not necessarily others): "This is not the way I choose to spend my time." In one respect, time is like money. If you decide to spend one hour doing one thing, you are choosing not to spend that hour on anything else. However, unlike money, when the hour is spent, it is not returnable. It is ironic how carefully we guard our money and how casually we guard our time.

Identify your "time robbers," those unimportant activities that take your time without giving a good return.

There are many sources of time wasters. Some common ones are:

- **Electronics** – too much time with television, IPods, telephones, computer games.
- **Indecision** – think about it, worry about it, and/or put it off.
- **Inefficiency** – doing things before thinking about the best way to do them.
- **Procrastination** – postponing until later.
- **Interruptions** – people dropping in, phones ringing, etc.
- **Errors** – working too fast or without enough information.
- **Crisis Management** – not planning ahead.
- **Poor organization** – wasting time looking for things not in their place.
- **Micro-management** – not properly delegating.
- **Perfectionism** – save perfection for the tasks that really need it.

You can easily waste as much time avoiding a project as you spend doing it. Put yourself into a routine for the jobs you have to do every day. Choose a specific time to answer your e-mail, complete paperwork, and plan your day. Use a calendar to keep you on target. Don't say "yes" to too many things, and don't commit to unimportant activities no matter how far in the future they may be.

The ways you are wasting time today are similar to the ways you have wasted time in the past. The only way it will change in the future is for you to take control of how you spend it. The more time we spend on planning and organizing a project, the less total time is required to do it.

A book I would recommend on time management would be Hyrum W. Smith's book, *The 10 Natural Laws of Successful Time and Life Management*. His definition of a natural law is a law that cannot be repealed. It works whether we want it to or not. It works whether we believe it will or not. It is like gravity; if you let go of something, it will fall – period. He divided his ten laws into five laws on managing your time and five laws on managing you life. I will list here the five laws he selected for time management exactly as he listed them in his book:

Law 1: You control your life by controlling your time.

Law 2: Your governing values are the foundation of personal success and fulfillment.

Law 3: When your daily activities reflect your governing values, you experience inner peace.

Law 4: To reach any significant goal, you must leave your comfort zone.

Law 5: Consistent daily planning leverages time and increases focus.

When Smith talks about "governing values," he is talking about priorities. Now that you recognize that you do have control over the way you spend your time, and it has become obvious from our priority list that many of the important things are not getting done, let's take a look at how to determine just what your priorities are.

"Start with the end in mind. Decide what you are going to do with the time, talent, and tools you have to work with." (Covey – Habit 2)

If we do not prioritize, we will end up doing first what appears to be urgent or what brings the most immediate pleasure or result. However, when we do prioritize, the things we do will line up with the things we feel are important; therefore, when we get them done, we feel better about the result. See the Time Use Chart on the next page.

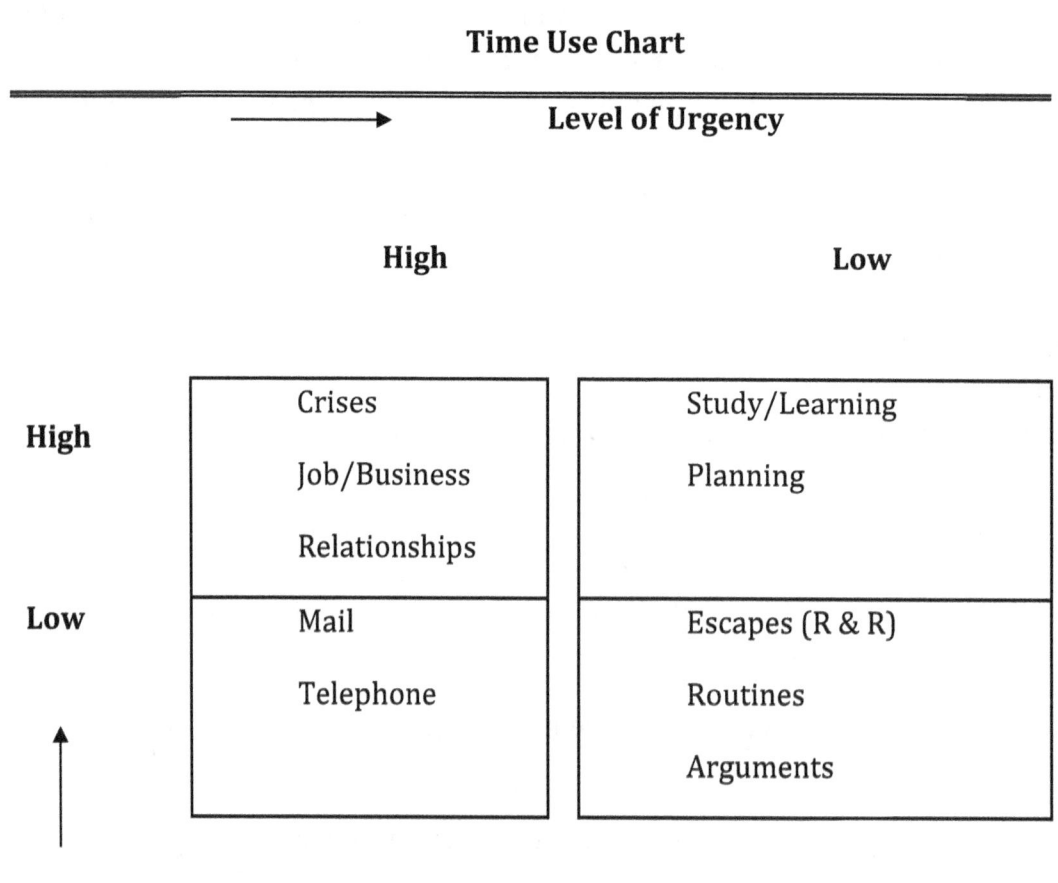

Important things are seldom urgent unless we make them so!

When you look at the above chart, you will see that the crises we face rate high in urgency and importance and planning rates high in importance but low in urgency. So, if we only handle the urgent problems, we will never get to the planning stage. Also, note that mail and telephone calls rate low in importance but high in urgency, which means we are doing the unimportant things on an urgent basis. If we plan, we can work in some R&R, which is rated low in importance and urgency, and control some of the crises by having plans in place to solve problems before they arise.

We have a tendency to overestimate what we can accomplish in one day and underestimate what we can accomplish in a year. As a result, most managers have more to do in one day than can be done. We have listed below a few guidelines to help you maintain control of your day:

1. Read selectively. You are responsible for what you put into your mind. If you have articles come across your desk on topics that directly relate to your ability to do your job, either read them and then file them appropriately or file them for later reference in a temporary file where they can be found easily – then take the time once a month to clean out the file of anything that is not going to be read. Control your leisure reading so that it does not interfere with your work time.

2. Have a prioritized, daily "to-do" list. How else will you ever stay focused?

3. Have a place for everything and take the time to put it there. This will save lots of search time later.

4. Do your task in order of importance.

5. Do one important thing at a time – several trivial things together.

6. Make a list of 5 to 10 minute tasks – phone calls, notes, etc. – to work on in wait times.

7. Break down large projects into bite-size pieces.

8. Know your critical 20% tasks – those tasks that are going to make the greatest difference in your success.

9. Save your best work time for the more important matters (the 20% tasks).

10. Schedule some private time without interruptions.

11. Don't procrastinate. As NIKE says: "Just do it!"

12. Keep track of how you use your time.

13. Set deadlines for each task to be accomplished.

14. Use your car as a university – Become a "road" scholar. Listen to educational tapes when driving.

15. Do busy work at one set time in the day.

16. Finish at least one project every day.

17. Schedule personal time.

18. Don't worry about anything – either do something about it or forget it.

19. Have long-term objectives.

20. Work to improve your time management skills daily and allocate time to train your family to do the same.

The more of these rules you incorporate, the more organized you will be, the more work you will get done, the less stress you will endure, and the more likely those living or working with you and for you will follow suit and establish their own set of productive habits.

Interruptions

We cannot always eliminate interruptions, but we can reduce them and their duration. If someone comes to your home, meet them at the door. Don't offer a seat unless you want to prolong the meeting. If you are in a serious time crunch and don't have anyone else to answer the phone, allow the answering machine to take calls and call back when it is more convenient. When no interruptions are critical, put a message board outside your door. You might want to establish a habit for uninterrupted times.

Conclusion

A major challenge for many people is the tendency to help others. Large gains can be made by delegating what can be delegated and focusing on the most critical issues first. Start taking control of your time. Record everything in your planner and stick to your schedule. Don't forget to mark off rest and relaxation time for yourself. Plan to avoid extra work by being prepared and setting reasonable deadlines for each activity. Leave time to review the project before it is accepted.

Time Management Record

Time	Event	Time	Event
:00		:00	
:15		:15	
:30		:30	
:45		:45	
:00		:00	
:15		:15	
:30		:30	
:45		:45	
:00		:00	
:15		:15	
:30		:30	
:45		:45	
:00		:00	
:15		:15	
:30		:30	
:45		:45	
:00		:00	
:15		:15	
:30		:30	
:45		:45	

Time Management

Don't forget to schedule sleep time. Determine what you need to include in the schedule.

After Thoughts

This book was originally created for our homeless veterans (*of which there should never be even ONE*). It can be read from cover to cover; however, it is designed for you to pick and choose the topic you need for the day. I have read hundreds of books, spent months in research and hours in prayer in hopes that the information in each topic will be what you need.

I have attempted to acknowledge each quote to the best of my ability. If I have quoted from memory and not realized where it came from, I sincerely apologize. Most of what you have read has come from personal experience, mistakes of my own, and lessons learned the hard way.

In each chapter you will find both Biblical and secular quotes. Much of this work and these ideas come from these great minds. The Bible is my main source of reference, but each author is also a great source of information.

For any of you who are teaching for the homeless, addicted, or prison re-entry population, I pray you will find this material to be a beneficial resource for you.

Thank you for your efforts.

Kathi Boyle

Contact Information

I would love to hear your opinion of what you have read and how or if it affected your life. You can comment in my e-mail or on my website.

Thank you!

www.kathiboyle.com
kathiboyle@comcast.net

www.ingramcontent.com/pod-product-compliance
Lightning Source LLC
Chambersburg PA
CBHW080450170426
43196CB00016B/2754